Doc, I Needed You Last Night

THE COUNTRY VET

A. J. Day, DVM

Illustration by Robin Gulack

outskirtspress

DENVER, COLORADO

Dedication

I would like to dedicate this book to my wife, Mary Jane and our three children; Susan, Tom, and Jim. Without their encouragement, I might never have written this book.

Foreword

Practicing veterinary medicine in lightly settled east central Illinois was very different in the early 1960's than it is today. Iroquois county, although 900 square miles in area, had a population of less than thirty thousand people. Watseka, the largest town had a population of about 5500 and the only stoplights in the county.

In the early days of the practice, ninety per cent of my work was caring for farm animals. Near the end of the century, however, the trend had reversed. Ninety per cent of my practice involved dogs and cats in an animal hospital setting.

Initially, when on a farm call I communicated with the office via a two way radio. Often, when I called in after finishing at one farm, I would find out that I had another call a few miles down the road. Thus, many miles of driving were saved. My phone rang both at my office and my home, so I didn't miss any emergency calls at night.

Only two injectable antibiotics, penicillin and streptomycin, were available in the early days of my practice. One oral antibiotic, terramycin, was available for large and small animals. Three or four sulfa products were available for use in drinking water for treating cattle, swine and poultry.

Very few practices owned x-ray machines, and blood chemistry profiles were unheard of until the late 1960's.

The usual charge for a dog spay was around ten dollars. Seven or eight dollars was the average charge for a farm visit, and as many as fifteen calls might be made in a day.

In 1961, there were six practicing veterinarians in Iroquois County. All of us were general practitioners, meaning we treated both farm animals and pets.

Today, there are three practicing veterinarians in the county, two small animal practitioners and one mixed animal practitioner.

The livestock population of Iroquois is drastically reduced from when I opened my practice in 1961 – almost no dairy or swine farms. There are a few beef cow herds left, but most have them have gotten smaller.

The population of the county and towns has changed very little. We do have a few more stoplights, and we now have an interstate highway running through the western half of the county.

Practicing veterinary medicine is not only the healing of animals…it is also dealing with animal owners with many different and often colorful personalities.

For nearly forty years, I was able to do what I loved and my education prepared me for…care for and heal the animals God created.

Contents

The Big Red Automobile

Soon after I opened my practice in Watseka, I began seeing a white over red Lincoln Town Car on the highway when I was traveling to or from a farm call. No driver could be seen, and as big as the car was, it looked like a boat without a helmsman.

In about two weeks' time, I learned who the owner of the auto was when she phoned me to request that I come to her house to vaccinate a dog. The lady's name was Ella Dascher and she lived in town with her aging sheep, her old horse, and her dogs and cats. When I arrived at her house and saw the sheep and horse in a residential area, I wondered why that was permitted. I later learned that at one time the reigning mayor had informed her that she would have to get rid of her animals. She responded that there was no way she was going to part with her horse and sheep and, if he thought otherwise he was badly mistaken. Those aren't exactly the words I was told she used, but I thought I had better clean up her comments. She was allowed to keep her animals.

When I met the elderly lady, I knew why I couldn't see anyone driving the car. She was so tiny…less than five feet tall and very thin. I thought she probably had to look through the space in the steering wheel to see over the dashboard. I wondered if she needed pedal blocks taped to the brake and gas pedal the way blocks were taped to the pedals on children's tricycles when their legs were too short.

Apparently, she liked the way I handled her dog when I vaccinated him because she told me she would be calling me again. Again turned out to be about two days later when she phoned to say her horse was down and asked me to come get her up. I don't think the horse was unable to get up; I think she just didn't want to get up for Mrs. Dascher. When I snapped a lead rope onto the halter, made a clucking noise and gave a tug on the rope she readily got to her feet. After she had called me several times to get the horse on her feet, I figured out that if I waited about a half hour before responding to her call I wouldn't have to go because the horse would rise on her own. Then Mrs. Dascher would phone me and tell me not to come.

I don't have any idea how old the sheep were, but they were old. After an episode with a very difficult lambing case, I suggested to the lady that she either get rid of the ram or keep him separated from ewes.

The difficult lambing case was one in which I was presented with a lamb with eight legs. The forelegs were fused, meaning I was confronted with two right forelegs and two left forelegs. In addition, the legs were pointing to the rear of the lamb and couldn't be bent at the knees so that the feet could be brought out first.

Mrs. Dascher was in the barn (part of a two car garage) with me when I informed her that I would need to do an embryotomy to remove the dead lamb(s) from the ewe. She simply said, "that's quite all right, Doctor. I'll just have to turn my back."

An embryotomy is the cutting of a fetus into pieces in the womb to make it easier to deliver the dead body. It would be nearly impossible to get instruments along with my hands into the womb of an animal as small as a sheep, so it was necessary to use obstetrical wire to sever the limbs.

Obstetrical wire is a braided wire perhaps 3/32 of an inch in diameter and is manufactured specifically for the purpose for which I was going to use it. One must take great care when using the wire in a sawing manner so that the mother's uterus isn't damaged.

After removing the first pair of forelegs, I had more room to examine the lamb. It was then I discovered there were two heads as well, so I proceeded to saw through one of the necks near the body to remove a head. Eventually, I removed enough pieces of the lamb's body so that I was able to remove the remaining parts of the lamb.

When I had every part of the lamb laid out in the straw of the pen, I could see that half of the eight legs were gray and half were black. One of the heads was gray, and one was black. In addition, I could see two livers, two stomachs, etc., because of a fissure or opening in the abdominal wall. All parts were there for a set of twins…except for the body, and there was only one.

A malformation such as this is known as a schistosoma reflexus and is a rare and fatal congenital disorder and is primarily observed in ruminant animals.

One time when I was treating Mrs. Dascher's horse, she asked me, "How old do you think Lady is?" I have to admit I was never very good at "mouthing" a horse to tell its age, but as I peeled back the upper lip and looked at the third upper incisor, I could see that Galvayne's groove extended the length of the lateral surface of the tooth. I did know that Galvayne's groove shows up near the gum line when the horse is five years old, extends halfway down the tooth at fifteen years, and is all the way down at twenty.

So I turned to her and said, "twenty years."

She kind of snorted and said, "You're just like Dr. Owings, you don't know anything about horses…she can't be a day over nineteen."

Dr. Owings was a veterinarian who practiced in Milford, about ten miles south of Watseka, and had done some work for Mrs. Dascher between the time the previous veterinarian left and I came to town. I knew that Dr. Owings was a competent and fine veterinarian, but I suspected that anyone who didn't tell her the age she wanted to hear about the horse, "didn't know anything about horses."

Every year thereafter, Mrs. Dascher would call me at breeding time and say, "Dr. Day, that old buck's making eyes at those ewes again." I would then answer, "Then it's time to shut that old buck up in a pen."

Once when I was called to see Mrs. Dascher's horse for a lameness problem, I took Dr. Hampton with me so I could consult with him.

He and Mrs. Dascher got into a conversation about growing old, and she told him about getting out of her car to close the garage door. For some reason, the automobile moved forward and trapped her between the door and the bumper, breaking both her legs above the knees. She then proceeded to raise the hem of her skirt to show him the scars.

I swear he was so embarrassed his face turned so red he could have lit up the night had it been dark.

CHAPTER 2

Tasty Leaves

Within two weeks after opening my practice, I received a call from a Mr. Lawrence regarding a cow that was "down". In the vernacular of farmers, a "down" or "downer" cow means one that is lying down and is unable to rise to the standing position. Since it was nearly lunchtime, I told him that I would be at his farm around one p.m.

After receiving directions to the Lawrence farm, I ate lunch and then proceeded on my way to the farm. Since we had only recently moved to the area, I carefully followed the directions I had been given, lest I become lost.

The route given to me took me through the downtown area and past the grain elevator. Since it was October and the farmers were harvesting their crops, there were trucks loaded with grain and tractors pulling one or more grain laden wagons lined up along the right side of the highway. There were so many of the vehicles that the elevator owners employed a man to direct traffic at the entrance to the elevator scales. After the vehicle had been weighed and moved on to the unloading area, the man would stop traffic to allow the next tractor or truck to enter or leave the elevator property.

After wending my way past the elevator, I came to the downtown stores and shops. It was homecoming at the local high school, and many of the shop windows were decorated with slogans urging the Warrior football team to win their game that night.

Since I had played high school football, the sights of the windows brought back pleasant memories. Apparently, the local high school did not have a homecoming parade like we had. Wondering about the parade brought back the memory of one of our homecoming parades when my Future Farmers of America Chapter loaded a big Holstein cow on a flatbed semi-trailer and entered the parade with the slogan "Just an Udder Victory for MHS" or "It's in the Bag". To this day, I don't know how we kept that cow on the trailer except she was very docile. Keeping her on the trailer was not one of my worries though as I was a very scared seventeen year-old driving a semi-trailer truck for the first time. By the way, we won the prize for the "most original float."

As I had been instructed, I dutifully turned right at the fourth stop light and proceeded down Fifth Street. I also made the next two turns as I had been instructed to do and proceeded south. This route also took me past the high school, and I could see the marching band practicing for their halftime performance that night. This route also took me past Legion Park, a forty acre parcel of land owned by the local American Legion Post, which included a swimming pool, playground equipment, and a very good baseball diamond for use of the Legion sponsored team and the high school team, as well as picnic areas.

Proceeding on my route, I passed a large drainage ditch with redwing blackbirds perched atop the tips of some of the many cattails growing there. Drainage ditches were new to me as I had grown up on the western side of Illinois where the land was more rolling, and we didn't need ditches to drain the farmland. I soon learned that some of the land in this county was very low and marshy and couldn't be farmed without proper drainage. I have been told that in the northeastern part of the county, much of the land wasn't tillable until after World War I when many miles of ditches were dug.

To my right there were pastures, and at the rear of the pastures I could see trees growing along what I would later learn to be Sugar Creek.

There were many different species of trees, from the maples with their orange colored leaves to the oaks with their golden leaves and, of course, the cedar trees with their green colored needles. Some of the pastures were separated by a row of Osage orange, or as it is commonly known, hedge.

Osage orange bears a fruit, known as hedge balls, about the size of an orange. I was told that the Indians of the area had used the wood from the Osage orange plant to make their bows.

Farmers also used the wood from the plant for fence posts, and I have bent many a staple trying to drive them into the very hard wood.

Farther along the road, I saw the remaining stalks of a cornfield that had been harvested, and the rows of stalks resembled soldiers standing at attention on a parade ground. The low cut stems of a soybean field that had been harvested looked like the top of a man's head that was sporting a crew cut.

When I drove onto the Lawrence farmstead, I saw two elderly gentlemen standing under a tree. I stopped near them, got out of the car and introduced myself. The one who was Mr. Lawrence then introduced me to his friend, Mr. Stroger, who was the owner of the cow I was called to treat.

I guess I need to clarify what I mean by elderly gentlemen. I suppose these men were in their mid to late fifties. I was twenty-eight years old and any one over the age of fifty seemed old to me. Now that I'm nearly eighty, fifty doesn't seem all that old. Since my parents had taught me to respect my elders, I addressed both of them as mister.

I learned that the cow was not at the Lawrence place, but in a timber pasture half a mile back down the road, and I was told to follow them. So I retraced my way back to a small stand of timber with some grass growing among the trees. As we drove into the timbered space, I could see a Guernsey cow lying in some grass. She appeared to be alert.

I walked to the rear of the cow, took out my thermometer in preparation for checking her for a fever and noticed that her bowel movement was in the form of small pellets, not the soft, mushy consistency that a cow's manure usually is. In fact, it looked more like sheep manure.

Although I had graduated from veterinary college a mere four months before, I had seen this type of bowel movement in a cow that I had diagnosed as having anaplasmosis when I was employed by another veterinarian in a practice in central Illinois.

I immediately thought, "Here's where the kid veterinarian (because that's pretty much how I thought of myself in this situation) impresses these old gentlemen." I wrongly assumed that the cow was infected with anaplasmosis. When I checked the cow's temperature, it was 101 degrees. Hmm, normal. Should have been around 106 degrees.

Then I opened the lips of the cow's vulva, and the mucous membrane was pink. If the cow had anaplasmosis, the appearance would have been jaundiced. Hmm, normal. I walked around to the cow's head and looked for ticks. Hmm, no ticks. Ticks are the carriers of a rickettsial organism called Anaplasma marginale which infects the cow's blood when the animal is bitten by a tick. I was glad I hadn't opened my mouth and made a diagnosis when I saw the fecal pellets. I looked at the cow's eyes and they were reasonably clear, but as my face was near the cow's head, I detected a sweet odor to her breath.

Under the pretense of going to my car to get something (but really to collect my thoughts), I started to walk away. After I had gone a few steps, one of the men said something and I stopped to hear what he had to say. As I looked down, I saw that I was standing in the middle of a patch of white snakeroot plants.

I don't remember what was said to me, but using what I had been taught in my poisonous plants course in vet school - constipation, lethargy, weakness, and a sweet odor to the breath along with how to identify a white snakeroot plant - I had my diagnosis. "Your cow is suffering from white snakeroot poisoning," I said to the two men. "Unfortunately, there is no sure treatment, but I'm going to try something."

On my way back to my car, I carefully went over in my mind what I had learned in the poisonous plants class I had taken. I now remembered that the plant contained an alcohol, trematol, and that is where the sweet odor to the breath had come from. I also remembered that ingestion of this plant causes depression and constipation with which the cow was definitely affected. However, the drug also can cause trembling, a sign she did not exhibit. Stimulants and cathartics were suggested treatment. However, in this case I dare not use a cathartic because the cow was in her last three months of pregnancy and a strong laxative might cause her to abort the calf.

I finally settled on a treatment regimen of five hundred cc. of fifty percent glucose intravenously, a pound of a mild laxative pumped into the cow's stomach using a stomach tube and pump, an intramuscular injection of multi-B vitamins and four GMT boluses forced down her throat with a balling or pill gun. GMT stands for glucose, methylene blue and sodium thiosulfate --the universal treatment for poisoning in the cow, especially when there's no known effective treatment. Besides, the blue color gives the farmer the sense one is doing something for the cow.

After treating the cow and suggesting they bring her a bucket of water to drink if she wanted it, I told the two men I would return the next morning at ten a.m. to administer treatment to the cow again, and left for my next farm visit.

When I returned the next morning, the two men were waiting for me. The cow was still alive and appeared to be somewhat stronger and more alert. I repeated the treatment and left with an agreement to return the following morning at the same time.

I returned the following day to two old gentlemen with big smiles on their faces and a cow that was standing up and had even eaten a small amount of grain. This time, I gave the cow only the injection of B-vitamins and four GMT tablets with a balling gun. We agreed that if the cow were not completely normal the next day, Mr. Lawrence would phone me and I would return and treat the cow again.

Mr. Lawrence did phone the following morning but only to tell me that the cow was completely normal and how much he appreciated what I had done for her. Both men became clients until their deaths several years later.

I was confronted with several more cases of white snakeroot poisoning during my career as a veterinarian and I saved several animals, but I never had the luck I did with my first case. Never again was I able to successfully treat a hundred percent of the animals I saw with this problem.

White snakeroot poisoning is a problem in cattle and sheep since both are ruminants.

However, it doesn't affect horses and swine. Cattle will eat the plant in the summer if they are on heavily grazed timber pasture and snakeroot is about the only plant left to eat, or in the fall when grass is brown and dry, and the snakeroot plant is green and succulent.

Humans may also be affected by white snakeroot poisoning by drinking milk from cows that have ingested the plant. The poison, trematol, is passed in the milk from a cow that has eaten the white snakeroot plant, and since the poison is in the milk before the cow shows symptoms of the disease, humans may drink the milk before knowing that it is poisonous.

I have heard that in the 1800's there were instances of humans dying from what was known as "milk sickness" in a timbered area a few miles east of the town in which I practiced.

Abraham Lincoln's mother is reported to have died of "milk sickness." However the author of one of the books I have read about Lincoln stated she probably died of brucellosis contracted from drinking milk from an infected cow.

Brucellosis in the human is a debilitating disease and does not cause a person to die in a short period of time as does trematol poisoning, so I would suggest Mrs. Lincoln probably died from drinking milk from a cow that had been poisoned by the white snakeroot plant.

᠊ᠰᠰᠰ

Another poisonous plant that I encountered was deadly or black nightshade, although I don't believe I ever treated a case of poisoning by this plant. The animals were dead when I saw them, and all I could do was identify the plants for the farmer and recommend that he eradicate them.

᠊ᠰᠰᠰ

I did see several cases of poisoning from the trimmings of Japanese ewe shrubbery. Not knowing that the plant was poisonous, the farmer would throw the trimmings out in the barn lot. Although the leaves resemble needles, they are soft and apparently tasty because the animals readily eat them.

My first case of Japanese yew poisoning occurred when the twelve year-old son of one of my best dairy clients trimmed the shrubs around the house and threw the trimmings into the calf lot.

I received the call from the farmer about six-thirty a. m. It was twenty miles to the farm, and I must admit I probably broke the speed limit getting there.

As I recall, there were twenty-two calves in the pen. We were told by the professor who taught the course, Plants Poisonous to Livestock, that there is no specific treatment for the toxin of the Japanese yew plant. When I arrived, three of the calves were dead. I treated the rest of the calves with an injection of prednisolone and an injection of atropine sulfate. None of the other calves died, but none of them were showing signs of being poisoned from the ingestion of Japanese yew needles.

I guess I will never know if my treatment saved the calves or if the three that died were the only ones who consumed the poisonous plants.

᠊ᠰᠰᠰ

My next case of Japanese Yew poisoning occurred in beef cattle that were being fed for slaughter.

I was in the kennel room one morning treating some hospitalized patients when one of my employees came back and said, "There's a very excited man on the phone who wants to talk to you."

"Who is it?" I asked.

"He didn't say," she replied.

I went to the phone in the hallway, and when I answered it, an excited voice said, "I've got one dead, one dying, and one down."

"Whoa, Whoa, who is this?" I asked.

"It's Gary Beever, and I'm losing cattle. My uncle trimmed the shrubs at my Grandma's place and threw the trimmings over the fence into the pasture."

I had never been to Grandma Beever's place, so I had to ask for directions.

With the directions he gave me in mind, I grabbed some bottles of injectable atropine sulfate and dexamethasone and headed for my practice vehicle.

It took me about a half hour to drive to the farm where the afflicted animals were kept.

I was somewhat dismayed when I arrived at Grandma's farm. There was no place to corral any of the animals -- the barn had no doors and there were no gates to make a pen to surround the animals.

I treated the two animals that were down, although I doubted it would help them due to their weakened conditions.

That left one very active, one thousand-pound steer to catch. Gary said, "Doc, you get in the bed of my pickup with your lariat, I'll drive past the steer and you throw the rope over his head."

While that idea sounded good in theory, it didn't take into account what would happen when the steer reached the end of the rope with me holding on to the other end, or where I was going to tie the steer when I caught him. I had visions of flying through the air. However, my parents didn't rear a dummy (I hope), so I tied the end of my lariat to the hitch under the bumper with which all pickup trucks are equipped.

As it turned out, I didn't have to rope the steer on the move. We finally cornered him between the truck, a wire fence and a corn crib. The steer was on the driver's side of the truck when I threw the rope over his head. As soon as the steer felt the rope around his neck, he bolted around the front of the truck and plunged head first into the passenger side door. The head of a steer as big as this one can leave quite a dent in the door of a truck. Immediately after butting the door, the steer reversed his direction and went back to the other side of the truck. In doing so, the lariat caught under the arm of the left windshield wiper. I didn't realize a wiper arm was strong enough to hold a big animal, but it did.

The steer dropped to its knees, I jumped out of the pickup bed, gave him two injections in the rump, flipped the quick release honda on my lariat and climbed back in the truck bed. After shaking his head a few times, the steer got to his feet and walked away.

In addition to the loss of the animals, the cost to repair Gary's truck was sixteen hundred dollars.

ﾉﾉﾉﾑ

I was called once to certify that a five hundred pound calf had been killed by lightning.

I found that the calf had not been killed by lightning, but from eating the wilted leaves of a wild cherry tree that had been struck by lightning.

The wilted leaves of a wild cherry tree contain cyanide and the calf actually died of cyanide poisoning. Normal leaves of a wild cherry tree are not lethal, only the wilted ones.

CHAPTER 3

Special Deliveries

I answered the phone on the third ring at two o'clock in morning to hear the voice of Alf Scherer say, "Doc, I really need you bad! I've been trying to pull this calf since eleven o'clock. The feet are showing, but it just won't come."

Why, oh why, did cows, sows and mares decide to have their offspring in the wee hours? I think they just did it to punish me for some unknown past sin.

"Okay, Alf, I'll get dressed and get there as soon as I can."

I was thankful it was April instead of January because it is a lot easier to get out of bed in the middle of the night on a warm spring morning than to get out on a cold wintry morning.

The distance to Alf's dairy farm was about nine miles, and I made it in reasonably good time. He was standing near the milk house anxiously awaiting my arrival.

The only equipment I needed were my plastic obstetrical sleeves and lubricant. Alf already had all the equipment it would take to deliver the calf: OB chains, and a fetal extractor.

When I walked in the barn, I saw one worn out cow. She was lying down in the dairy barn with her head still in the stanchion. Alf had, however, opened the stanchion so she could move her head around.

While I was pretty certain I knew the problem, to make sure I inserted my right hand (covered with a plastic sleeve) past the two visible feet into the cow's vagina. It was then I felt two more feet. I thought, "This is interesting." Then I looked at the two feet outside the vulva. Yes, there was a left and a right. The only problem was the right foot was on the left and the left foot was on the right, the chain was on a foot of each calf. No wonder Alf couldn't "pull" the calf.

I rearranged the chains so that I had them on the legs from one calf and pushed the other calf back as far as I could. Then I asked Alf to hook up the "calf puller".

After placing the curved portion of the instrument around the cow's upper legs below the vulva, he extended the cable along the shaft and hooked it onto the chains. As I repelled the calf that wasn't hooked to the fetal extractor, Alf slowly turned the handle to reel in the cable. Gradually, the calf began to emerge from the birth canal. Once the head popped through the vulva, I grabbed the chain and pulled the calf the rest of the way out. Unfortunately, the calf was dead.

Alf quickly drug the dead fetus out of the way and handed me the chain. Forming loops in each end of the chain, I placed them around each foot. Then I sat down and placed my feet against the cow with my legs bent at the knees. Grasping the chain with two handles, I slowly straightened my legs, and the calf exited the vulva. It was an easy task to get the calf the rest of the way out. This calf was dead, too. The stress these calves had undergone during the three or so hours Alf had been unsuccessfully trying to deliver them had taken its toll.

I must say, the cow wasn't in very good shape either. After retrieving two bottles of electrolytes and an I.V. tube from my truck, we pulled her head out of the stanchion. Placing a nose lead in her nasal septum and pulling her head around, I inserted the needle and gave her the electrolytes. Then I suggested to Alf that he get her a pail of water.

The cow did survive and was up and eating the next morning.

Another call in the wee hours of the morning, from a swine producer this time, awakened me.

"I have a sow out here that is not having her pigs and need you to come out," said Cal Wooster.

It was seldom that I ever refused to make a call at any time of day or night if it was a true emergency, but I was so tired.

"Is she in a farrowing crate?" I asked.

"Yes."

"Get her out of the crate and walk her up and down the alleyway between the crates. If she doesn't start having pigs, call me back."

"Okay."

I climbed back into my bed and didn't remember the call until in the morning when I stopped at my favorite restaurant around ten o'clock for a cup of coffee.

Cal and his wife were having breakfast after church. He waved me over to his table and, as I approached, said, "Boy, that really worked. As she was walking up and down the aisle, the pigs just started dropping out. She had a litter of twelve."

Cal got his pigs without having to pay for a farm call, and I got a full night's sleep. We both were happy.

⁂

For once I can write about an obstetrical case that didn't require me to go out in the middle of the night. It was just as bad, however, as it occurred during my walk-in office hours. With ten people waiting for me to see their dogs and cats, I was called for a dystocia in a Belgian mare. I quickly explained to the waiting clients that it was a matter of life and death. If I didn't get to the farm to deliver the foal soon, the foal might die. There was a consensus of opinion that I should go…they would wait until I returned.

I drove the twelve or so miles to Rosewood Farm in record time, flew into the barnyard, and slammed on my brakes. Nothing is as impressive as a veterinarian flying to the rescue of one of a prized group of mares. Right?

The mare was in a small pasture next to the house. As I walked up to her, she strained, and a small amount of fluid dripped from her vulva.

"What have you seen?" I asked.

"Just what you saw now, but no feet," replied Mrs. Rosewood. Mr. Rosewood didn't seem to be around, but I didn't ask his whereabouts. The twelve year-old son was on hand to help me pull the foal if necessary. It is a "no, no" to use a fetal extractor on a mare.

I placed a twitch on the horse's upper lip and gave the handle to Mrs. Rosewood, who already was holding a lead rope in her other hand. Then I slipped my sleeved and lubricated arm into the mare's vagina. What I felt wasn't what I had hoped to feel. Instead of two front feet and a nose, I felt two hocks. The foal was breech. This would be a real challenge for me as the mare was about fifteen hands high and weighed nearly a ton. My arms are thirty-two inches long. I decided that I needed an equalizer…a general anesthetic. This would stop the mare from straining, and would relax her so that the foal, if I ever got the legs extended, would be easier to deliver.

I injected the anesthetic intravenously and within seconds the mare dropped easily to the ground and rolled over on her right side. That was good for me, as I am right handed. Down on my knees, I inserted my hand into the vagina and grasped one of the hocks and tugged on it to bring the lower leg farther back so I could try to grasp the foot. The mare's cervix was widely dilated, which should make delivery easier. Starting at the hock, I worked my way down to the foot and began to bring it to the rear. Finally, I brought the first foot through the cervix, and then the other one. Then I placed loops of nylon obstetrical strap around the lower legs, just above the hooves.

Sitting down behind the mare with my legs bent, I slowly started to straighten my legs. It was a difficult pull, so the Rosewood boy sat down beside me and helped me. I thought we might have to ask Mrs. Rosewood to help as well. Slowly, more of the foal's rear legs began exiting the vulva. Once we had the big hips to the exterior, one good pull, and the rest of the foal came easily. The foal snorted a couple of times, blew his nose (no handkerchief) and began to breathe normally.

Two things happened about that time...the mare started to wake up and Mr. Rosewood came sauntering across the pasture. I don't know which was the more exciting, seeing the mare come around, or hearing Mrs. Rosewood tear into Mr. Rosewood.

"Where in the h--- have you been?"

"I just went into town for a little while."

"A little while...I got home at one o'clock, and you were gone then. It's now nearly five."

About that time, the mare rose to her feet and I said, "I've got clients waiting for me at the office," picked up my equipment and headed for my truck.

I never heard who won the fight, but my bet was on Mrs. Rosewood.

When I arrived back at my office, nine of my ten clients were still there and another three had been added. I worked a little overtime that night.

♪♪♪♪

The first few years in practice, I did a lot of work on dairy farms. Most of the cows I treated were Holsteins...big black and white cows. A few farmers milked Guernseys and a few milked Jerseys. The Holsteins gave more gallons of milk than the other two breeds, but the butterfat content of the milk was not as high. In other words, the milk from Holsteins was not as rich.

Providing veterinary service for dairy farmers meant being called early in the morning or around supper time (or dinnertime, whichever you prefer), as that was when they did their milking. And so it was when a farmer of German extraction called me to deliver a calf one morning...from a Guernsey cow.

There were two feet protruding slightly from the vulva when I arrived at the farm. I could see just the tips of two hooves. As I prepared to deliver the calf I noticed a peculiar odor emanating from the cow's vagina. Putrefaction! This cow had been trying to have her calf for a few days, and the calf was dead.

When I inserted my hand into the vagina, I was certainly glad I had a plastic sleeve on it, or I would have carried a very bad smell around with me for quite a while. I could change my coveralls if they became smelly and soiled, but not my skin.

Soap didn't work too well to remove the odor, either.

The first things I felt when I entered the cow's vagina were two more feet, but they were farther back than the first two. We had a pair of dead twins. I placed the loops of the obstetrical strap around the front legs just above the hoof. Tightening the loops, I started pulling on the strap with my right hand. With my left, I attempted to repel the head of the other calf. Gradually, the first calf began to come through the birth canal. Once I got the head through the vulva, I brought my left hand out so I had two hands to pull with.

When about half of the odorous calf was out of the cow, the farmer gulped and said, "I need some schnapps," and headed for the bottle he kept in the milk house. For the uninitiated, a milk house is where the milk taken from the cows is kept in a refrigerated tank until the milk truck comes to haul it off each day. In fact, it is pumped directly from the milking machines to the tank.

I delivered the first calf, and when I had the second calf about half way out, Walter returned to the barn. Taking one whiff of the smelly calf, he gulped and said, "I need some more schnapps," and headed back to the milk house.

After placing two sulfa boluses deep in each uterine horn and giving the cow an injection of penicillin, I took my pail into the milk house to get some warm water to wash my equipment.

Walter was still in the milk house, looking a little pale. He asked, "Want some schnapps?"

"Not at seven o'clock in the morning, Walter."

He then wrote me a check for my services.

After reminding him to let me know if the cow did not pass two afterbirths in the next forty eight hours, I got in my truck and went on my merry way to my next call.

And then I began to wonder. If the odor of the dead calf affected Walter so much when he was six feet from it, how would it affect him when he had to bury the calves?

꩜꩜꩜

We owned a small farm on which I raised feeder pigs to sell to farmers to fatten for the market.

There was room in the farrowing house for twenty four sows, so we bred twelve sows each month. When we weaned one batch of pigs, twelve sows were removed from the farrowing house, and twelve new ones moved in.

I would arise early each morning and drive the five miles to the farm to feed the sows and check on them and the pigs. If a sow was giving birth to pigs, I might check her later in the day, or not until I fed the sows in the evening.

One morning, I found a big Hampshire sow in labor, so I kept an eye on her as I was working around the farrowing house. When I arrived that morning, she had four live pigs in the crate with her. When I was finished feeding the sows, she had six. She seemed to be doing fine, so I left for the office.

I was scheduled to make a farm call in the area of our farm at nine o'clock so I would stop in to check on the sow at that time.

When I stopped in to see the sow again while on my farm call, there were twelve baby pigs in the crate with the new mother, but there was no afterbirth. This meant she probably had more pigs to be born. However, I figured she was about done and I needn't check on her until evening when I fed the sows again.

After closing my office at six o'clock in the evening, I once more drove to the farm to do my evening chores. As usual, when I turned on the light in the farrowing house, all the sows but one jumped to their feet and wanted to be fed. Before filling the feed cart, I walked to the crate where the new mother lay and started counting. Eighteen pigs!!

It was great for us to have the eighteen pigs except…the sow had only twelve nipples. Fortunately, we had two or three new mothers who had more nipples than pigs, so I could place some of the pigs with those mothers.

After I fed the sows, I spread some of the new pigs around to other sows. In the end, sixteen of the eighteen pigs survived.

⟫⟫⟫⟫

Another early morning call summoned me to one of the standard bred horse farms to deliver a foal. Mandy Roberts had gotten me out of bed and excitedly told me that the mare they had sent to Kentucky to be bred to that expensive stallion was in labor, and she would like me to come out.

When I arrived I was told the water bag had broken about an hour ago, but nothing was happening.

I examined the mare to discover the foal was in the breech position.

After anesthetizing the mare I got down behind her on the floor and was able to straighten the legs and bring the feet outside the mare. Then, with the use of some pulling power, we delivered a live colt.

Mandy was excited and said, "Doc, I think I'll name that colt A. J. Day." She did that, and I don't know if that name jinxed the colt or not, but he never turned out to be much of a racehorse. I was hoping that he would go on to race at the Meadowlands, or some other large track, and through him my name would become famous. But, alas, that didn't happen.

⟫⟫⟫⟫

"Dr. Day, I'm confused," said Ken South when I answered the phone.

"And, why is that, Ken?" I asked.

"I've got twelve cows, and last night I had twelve calves. This morning I have thirteen calves, and one of them is newborn."

"Did one cow have a pair of twins?"

"No, each cow had one calf nursing her last night."

"I believe you have a rarity, Ken. One of your cows conceived a second time even though she was already carrying a calf. How old are the other calves?"

"About two months."

"Apparently, your cow ovulated, was bred, and conceived a second time. You have a pair of twins of different ages. This is called superfetation and is a rare phenomenon. I'm surprised that the cow didn't abort the younger calf when she gave birth to the first."

"Are you still confused?" I asked Ken.

"Yes, but not as much as I was," he answered.

The cow raised both calves.

ↄↄↄↄ

"I've just been out to Tom Warren's farm to see his triplet calves," said the local newspaper reporter. "How is that cow going to feed all three of those calves?"

"Well, Tom feeds his cattle well, and she'll produce enough milk for the three of them. If not, the calves will either rob from other cows, or Tom can bucket feed them with milk replacer."

The reporter then said, "Let me see, the mother is a Charolais crossbred cow, and her husband is a purebred Angus."

"You have the breeds right, but they're not married. Those calves are illegitimate. The cow was sort of pasture bred," I said, not realizing all this would appear in the next issue of the paper. I thought the reporter would know that I was just kidding her.

The next time I saw Tom, I attempted to apologize to him, but he thought what I said about the cow and bull was funny.

He did thank me for the complement I paid him on the care of his cattle.

ↄↄↄↄ

Jim Tuggle, one of my favorite clients, was a bachelor who lived with his widowed mother on her farm. He was really laid back and nothing seemed to bother him. Mrs. Tuggle was a wonderful cook, and usually invited me in for cookies or cake and coffee when I was at their farm. Perhaps that is the reason Jim was a favorite client.

I was having a particularly difficult time delivering a calf because

I couldn't reach the feet. The muscles of the left side of the cow were relaxed and stretched out and the uterus was lying on the floor of the abdomen. The cow was not contracting her uterus to propel the calf toward the cervix, and my arms were shorter than I needed them to be to reach the calf.

A neighbor, Will Wayne, was there for the delivery because the cow was bred to his new bull, and this would be the first calf born that the bull had sired.

Will was making comments such as, "I can't wait to see that calf...I'll bet he's a big one," and "hurry up Doc, I want to see that big calf."

Finally, I was able to get a hold on one of the forelegs and pull the calf farther back toward the cervix. Then, I managed to get hold of both feet with one hand and bring the calf back far enough to get an obstetrical strap on both feet and deliver the calf.

When the calf hit the floor of the barn, I thought Will Wayne was going to faint. Instead of the huge calf that he had been talking about, I had delivered a calf that was about fifteen inches tall and weighed about twenty-five pounds.

Jim Tuggle was laughing, and Will Wayne had nothing to say. He was speechless for probably the only time in the forty-five years I knew him.

I don't know why the calf was so small, but I do know the old cow was way past her prime. Had she been able to contract her uterus, she would have popped that small calf out with no trouble.

After she weaned the calf, it was off to the slaughter house for her.

꩜꩜꩜

I was once called to deliver a calf from a cow that was lying down in a mud hole in the alleyway of a corncrib. You ask, "Why was there a mud hole in the middle of a building with a roof?" The answer: "There was a big hole in the roof, and it had been raining for several days."

As I walked behind the Angus cow, I could see the tip of the nose and two feet peeking out of the vulva. I had carried my fetal extractor, and the other necessary instruments and tools needed to deliver a calf, into the crib from my practice vehicle.

Kneeling behind the cow and trying to keep out of the mud, I started to place the loops of the OB strap around the forefeet of the calf.

Suddenly I heard, "You're going to have to cut that calf up to get him out." Apparently some veterinarian had done an embryotomy on a calf in order to deliver it sometime, and he thought that was the only way to get the calf out. As pointed out in another chapter in this book, an embryotomy is the dismemberment of a fetus in the uterus or the vagina to facilitate delivery that is impossible by natural means.

I looked up at the owner and said, "No, I can deliver him whole."

He retorted with, "I said you'll have to cut him up."

Since I believed my knowledge about delivering a baby calf was superior to his, I picked up my equipment and started for my truck.

"Where are you going?" he asked.

"Home," I replied, "If you know more about delivering a calf than I do, you might as well do it."

He then said, "Do it your way."

With the use of the fetal extractor, I had the calf out in no time.

Throwing a loop of my lariat over the cow's head, I started to pull and encourage the cow to get to her feet. However, it wasn't as easy as it seemed…the cow was standing belly deep in that mud hole. It took quite an effort for the two of us to pull her out of that quagmire.

CHAPTER 4

Shipping Fever

I was at Rob Pierce's farm treating a Holstein dairy cow for mastitis (inflammation of the udder) when he said, "Doc, when we're finished here I would appreciate it if you would run over to the Franzen place on the highway and take a look at some feedlot steers. We just got a new shipment of cattle in, and I don't like the way they look." Rob had no monetary interest in the cattle, but was paid by the owner to feed them and see to their well-being.

I followed Rob to the feedlot about two miles away, and when I walked into the barn where the cattle were, I could tell we had big troubles so far as their health was concerned.

As I walked around among the cattle, I could see matter in the corners of inflamed eyes on many of them. In addition, many were coughing and breathing roughly. A thick ropy discharge hung from the noses of most of the calves.

"Rob, you've got some very sick cattle here," I said.

"You think they've got shipping fever, Doc?" he asked.

"No doubt," I answered.

Shipping fever is a common term for respiratory disease in newly acquired cattle that are purchased for the purpose of fattening them for slaughter. Several viruses and bacteria may be involved in the disease process. Among the viruses known to be involved are

Parainfluenza 3 Virus (PI3) and Infectious Bovine Rhinotracheitis Virus (IBR). Pasteurella, bacteria that cause pneumonia, may also be involved. Since some of the cattle had diarrhea, I also had to consider Bovine Viral Diarrhea.

Shipping fever, or the bovine respiratory disease complex, is common in cattle that pass through a consignment sale barn where several farmers bring small numbers of feeder calves to sell.

A cattle dealer may buy two or three different groups and put them together because he has a farmer with a cattle feedlot that he needs to stock. At the same time, another dealer may have purchased two or three groups of calves and put them together to sell to the same farmer. Some of the calves may have one of the diseases and some may have another disease. When you put all the groups together, the viruses or bacteria start batting around through the whole herd. The way the disease agents explode and spread from one calf to another is kind of like watching fireworks on the 4th of July.

I recommended to Rob that I take swabs of material from the calves' noses and eyes and send them to the University of Illinois Diagnostic Lab for culturing. Then we would know just what we were dealing with and have an idea of how to treat the calves.

Rob replied that the owner, Jack Franzen, would be coming from Champaign the next morning and asked me to be at the farm at nine o'clock to meet with him.

I made it to the farm at nine o'clock, but had to wait for Mr. Franzen. When he did arrive he wasn't very cordial and wanted to know what was happening with the cattle.

I explained in detail what examination of the calves had revealed to me and what diseases I suspected. I also suggested taking the swabs and sending them to the lab. He said, "I live in Champaign, and I can take them right back with me when I go home." I replied, "That would be great. I won't even have to pack the swabs in ice."

I then told him that my wife's parents lived in Champaign, and he asked their names.

When I told him, he said, "Why, I know Max. He and I go to Kiwanis Club together."

I then took swabs from the eyes, nose and rectum of several of the calves, labeled them and packed them in a box of cotton so there would be no breakage. Since I thought Mr. Franzen was going to transport the samples directly to the lab, I didn't pack them in ice.

I was sure the veterinary diagnostician would phone me the next day, but that didn't happen. However, the following day, just as I was about to phone the lab, the veterinarian at the lab phoned me.

The results were pretty much as I expected. IBR, PI3, and Pasteurella species had been isolated from the nasal and ocular discharges. Dr. Randall, the veterinary pathologist asked me, "Why did you take rectal swabs?" I replied that the owner and his nephew, for whom I did veterinary work on two other farms, questioned everything I told them so I wanted to cover all bases. He replied that the calves must be really sick, because respiratory viruses are seldom recovered from the feces. Viruses were recovered from the feces from these calves, however.

When I told the pathologist that I had hoped to hear from him the previous day, he replied that he hadn't received the samples until the previous day. He said Mr. Franzen told him he took the samples with him to Chicago and returned to Champaign the following day.

I was really surprised that the lab was able to isolate any viruses considering the swabs were not packed in ice, which would allow them to deteriorate more rapidly.

I phoned Rob Pierce to tell him that I had the results, and he said I should phone Mr. Franzen's nephew, George. According to Rob, George was going to treat the cattle and vaccinate them. I wasn't disappointed to hear this as I knew if I treated them I would be subjected to criticism and second guessing.

Seeing this group of sick cattle reminded me of when I took my oral state board exam to practice veterinary medicine in Illinois. I was asked just two questions: Would I open my own practice or be employed by another veterinarian, and how would I handle an outbreak shipping fever in a group of cattle?

After telling the questioners I would be employed by another veterinarian, I explained that I would isolate the sick calves and treat them. Then I would vaccinate the ones who were not sick.

My answers must have satisfied them, because they then said, "Thank you, you're finished." I was really surprised, because some of my classmates were questioned for more than half an hour.

***

The father of one of my clients passed away and left three farms to him and his two brothers.

After selling two of the farms, they decided to go into the cattle finishing business. By cattle finishing, I mean they would purchase calves and feed them up to slaughter weight.

The building they constructed had a ventilation system and a slotted floor so the manure produced by the cattle would be pushed through the slots to a pit below. The urine from the cattle would keep the manure in a semi liquid state so that it could be pumped into a big tank wagon and spread on the farm ground as fertilizer.

My client's experience with feeder cattle amounted to zero. Up to now, his cattle raising experience was limited to about ten Hereford cows whose calves he sold to other farmers to feed for market.

I don't know who advised them on what size calves to buy or even if they had any advice. Either way, they picked the wrong sized calves for beginners to try to feed for slaughter.

The first time I was summoned to treat cattle I learned that the brothers had purchased four hundred calves with an average weight of three hundred pounds each. Three hundred pounds is an ideal weight for calves to get really sick when they go through a sale barn or two, or three.

Had my advice been sought, I would have recommended they purchase six hundred pound cattle for an inexperienced person to start a cattle feeding operation. But, alas, my advice was not asked for.

And that's why I spent forty five consecutive days on that farm treating sick calves, missing Fighting Illini football games for which I had tickets, missing church on Sundays, and who knows what else.

I called in the beef cattle experts from the College of Veterinary Medicine at the U of I, hoping they could recommend better treatment methods than I was using. They took samples back to the lab and phoned me saying my treatment regimen was fine, but due to the seriousness of the disease outbreak, we should expect sixty-five of the calves to die.

When all was said and done, we lost only sixteen calves.

❧❧❧

Another one of my clients, Gary Hockley, had fed cattle all the years he had been farming, and he did a good job of it.

However, his cattle got sick on occasion. Gary would go as far as he could in treating them for respiratory disease, and then he would call me.

He always said, "I treat the easy ones, Doc, for the hard ones, I call you."

I don't remember the exact year, but it was in the 1980's, when we had a very bad cold snap around Christmas time. In addition, we had a lot of blowing snow and some of the roads were blocked. Those that weren't blocked were hazardous on which to drive.

I was treating several newly acquired calves for Gary and intended to go to his farm early on Christmas morning. I believe the wind chill factor was minus twenty- five degrees on Christmas Eve. Several church services were cancelled due to the cold.

When I tried to go to Gary Hockley's farm on Christmas morning, the police had the highways blocked and wouldn't let me out of town.

All day, I tried to phone Gary but couldn't get through because all the lines were busy. Finally, I reached him at seven o'clock that night and explained why I didn't get to his place that day.

He said, "Oh, that's all right, I didn't expect you. I sure hope you can make it tomorrow though."

CHAPTER 5

Dr. Hampton

I would be remiss if, in the writing of this book, I did not mention Dr. Richard Hampton.

On the day after moving to Watseka I called on Dr. Hampton, an elderly veterinarian, who was still conducting a limited practice. He was in his yard when I drove up and parked in front of his house.

Dr. Hampton was a wizened little man, perhaps five feet five inches in height, and weighing around one hundred ten pounds, or even less. I could not envision him conducting a practice involving large draft horses, but he started practice long before most farmers owned tractors.

After I introduced myself, we sat down on the grassy bank next to his sunken driveway. As we were talking, I offered him a Camel cigarette. He said, "Oh, you smoke 'tailor mades' (meaning manufactured cigarettes)." He accepted the cigarette from me and said he had always "rolled his own."

We had an interesting conversation about the practice of veterinary medicine. I found that not only was he very intelligent, but that he was also well read and up to date on animal diseases and veterinary techniques.

Abruptly, he asked, "Do you intend to make Sunday calls?" My answer was, "If I provide veterinary service for a client during the week, I will certainly see their animals on Sunday if it's an emergency."

"Good", he said. "Your predecessor didn't make Sunday calls, so his clients always called me." He was referring to the veterinarian who had previously practiced in Watseka, but who had moved on to a staff job at the University of Illinois.

Without my asking him, he proceeded to give me a history of his life as a veterinarian. He had graduated from Chicago Veterinary College -- I believe he said in 1913. Initially, he had settled in a small town west of Watseka.

When the United States entered World War I, he volunteered for the U. S. Army Veterinary Corps. He attained the rank of Captain and served as the Assistant to the Chief Veterinarian of the American First Army, Lieutenant Colonel Louis A. Merillat. Dr. Merillat had served as Dean of Chicago Veterinary College when Dr. Hampton was a student.

Returning from military service in 1919, he purchased a practice in another town near Watseka from a veterinarian who wanted to move to Florida. As he told the story, within a year the veterinarian in Florida began writing him wanting him to sell the practice back to him. Dr. Hampton said the previous practice owner was so persistent that he finally gave in and resold the practice.

He then moved to Watseka where he was still conducting a limited practice when I moved to town. Apparently he was satisfied that I was going to treat clients in a way which he approved of, because it wasn't long before he retired.

While I was visiting him, I noticed that he was wearing a small black leather bow tie which, according to people who knew him well was part of his normal attire and was his trademark-- even when making farm calls.

Before I left his place, he had to show me the equipment in the trunk of his 1953 Ford automobile. He still carried about the same equipment I carried in my station wagon. He also said I should call him Dick, but I told him I would rather call him Dr. Hampton, if he didn't mind. He smiled when I said that, so I believe he was pleased by my respect.

Learning that I had served in the U. S. Navy during the Korean War, he signed me up as a member of Watseka American Legion Post 23 that day.

I must say that I took full advantage of Dr. Hampton's knowledge and experience, especially in regard to horses.

Once when I had an appointment to castrate a horse with a testicle that had not descended into the scrotum (commonly known as a high flanker), I asked him to go with me in case I needed his advice while doing the surgery.

Fortunately for me, the surgery went off without a hitch and I did not need any help from Dr. Hampton. When I finished, he said, "You did a great job for never having done that surgery before." I replied, "To tell you the truth, Doctor, I've probably performed the surgery three or four times, but didn't know what I was dealing with."

I did learn one thing new that day. Dr. Hampton taught me how to throw a horse on an army blanket. By placing a loop of the rope around a horse's neck and the two ends of the rope around the rear ankles, back through the loop and pulling, one can drop a horse to the ground in an area the size of an army blanket.

He said. "That's how we did it in WWI."

Another time, when I was called to treat a lame horse, knowing that I was limited in the knowledge of the cause and treatment of lameness in horses, I asked him to consult with me. He seemed to enjoy these moments of brotherhood with a fellow veterinarian. In this case, he diagnosed ringbone of the joint just above the hoof, and volunteered to mix up a "blister compound" for me to use in treating the condition. The ointment he mixed consisted of red mercuric acid, cantharides powder, and lard. His instructions were to apply the mixture to the swelling and bandage the lower leg, with removal of the bandage after four days. When I removed the bandage, the eighteen year old horse was greatly improved.

I was called on a Sunday night to treat several litters of baby pigs for severe scours (diarrhea) by a farmer who had previously been a client of Dr. Hampton's.

I don't recall exactly how long it took me to treat all the pigs, but I know I was there for over two hours. In addition, I left medicine with the farmer to use to continue treatment of the pigs.

When I sent the farmer a bill for my services at the end of the month, he immediately went to Dr. Hampton with it and told Dr. Hampton that he thought I had overcharged him. "No," Dr. Hampton said, after he had studied the statement, "I don't think he charged you enough."

Once I was called to replace a vaginal prolapse in a Hereford cow owned by another former client of Dr. Hampton's.

A vaginal prolapse is a condition in which the wall of the vagina is pushed out through the vulva and looks like a pink ball under the cow's tail. Sometimes that pink ball can approach the size of a basketball, especially if it is filled with the cow's urinary bladder.

An overly fat cow carrying a large calf is predisposed to this condition.

When I walked into the barn, I saw that the barn had not been cleaned in quite some time. The wet manure was about eight inches deep.

After roping the cow and tying her to the manger, I said, "Please get some straw--I wouldn't put a well cow in this barn, let alone a sick one."

He replied, "You're just like Dr. Hampton. He always wanted a clean place to work, too."

When I later related the incident to Dr. Hampton, he said, "If I were you, I'd consider that a compliment."

Occasionally on a Sunday afternoon, my family would make ice cream. I recall when I was a child, before three of my brothers and two brothers-in-law went off to serve during World War II, our entire family gathered at my parents' home on Sunday afternoons and made home-made ice cream.

This was the late 1930's and early 1940's and we had to turn the crank that made the paddles go to freeze the ice cream. Now, we were modern, no physical labor was required -- the paddles were turned by electricity.

I phoned Dr. Hampton on one of the "ice cream" Sunday afternoons and asked if he liked home-made ice cream. He responded by asking, "Do you happen to be old fashioned enough to use cream instead of milk in the ice cream?"

"You betcha," I replied. "I went to one of my clients and got cream from Jersey cows yesterday, so the ice cream will be extra rich."

"We'd love to have some good home-made ice cream," he said.

About an hour later, I delivered some ice cream to Dr. & Mrs. Hampton and they were very pleased.

At Christmas time that year, Dr. Hampton brought a cake to my hospital and said, "Here's a Christmas present for your family."

When I took the cake home and we opened the box it was in, we could see that the cake was only about one inch high…it had failed to rise when he baked it. He had however gone to the trouble of decorating the white icing with red and green sprinkles.

After we had eaten the cake, I phoned Dr. Hampton to thank him and tell him how good the cake was.

I could tell that he was pleased that I had called to thank him and compliment him on the cake. His response was a modest, "I made it myself."

One winter we had a very heavy snow and I knew I would not be able to make any farm calls until all the roads were cleared. My primary concern was to clean the driveway and sidewalks at home, and then the parking lot and walks at my animal hospital. I knew I could call on a high school student who worked part-time for me. If all went well, I would open my office in the afternoon.

I was sure Dr. and Mrs. Hampton were snowed in, so I asked my wife, Mary Jane, to phone them to see if they needed anything from the grocery store or if they would like for us to clean their sidewalks and driveway of snow.

Mrs. Hampton replied they were good with the groceries and said Dick would shovel the snow.

I knew that "Dick" was over eighty years of age and didn't need to be shoveling snow, so I loaded the high school student and my older son, Tom, into the car and we went to clean the sidewalks and driveway for the Hamptons.

When I saw the shovel that Dr. Hampton had to work with, I decided that the snow would melt faster than he could shovel it. The shovel wasn't much bigger than the shovel we used to remove the ashes out of the bottom of the coal fired heating stove when I was a child. In fact, the shovel was just the right size for my eight year old son.

After we finished the job at Dr. Hampton's, he said, "I'm glad you did this. I just remembered that I have an appointment downtown this afternoon. I wouldn't have been able to get out of my driveway."

Dr. Hampton sometimes brought newspapers to my hospital for me to use in my dog and cat cages. Since he only brought a small stack about three inches thick each time, I always thought he used this as a reason to come and spend time with me in my hospital.

It gave him a chance to talk veterinary medicine and commune with a fellow veterinarian.

Once, when he brought a small stack of papers, I asked about Mrs. Hampton. He replied, "Doctor, she's sick but, you know, she's been sick ever since I have known her." He hesitated a bit and then said, "I think it's a neuroses."

I feel that I probably gained more from our friendship than Dr. Hampton did. To me, his age and experience were invaluable when I asked him for guidance and advice.

I learned quite a lot about Dr. Hampton from his former clients. He had an English Bulldog, named Clinker, who rode with him in his Model T Ford with side curtains that he drove on his farm calls. I was told that Clinker would sit right up in the passenger seat just as a human would. Apparently, Dr. Hampton had treated a sick Clinker for an itinerant prize fighter who happened to be passing through town. When the owner did not have enough money to pay the bill, he gave the dog to Dr. Hampton.

Dr. Hampton did tell me that he had played football on the Chicago Veterinary College football team. He said his position was end -- imagine a five foot five, one hundred and ten pound man playing on a college team today. I was also told that he attended the practices of the local high school football team where he volunteered as a coach.

I still fondly remember the times I spent with Dr. Hampton.

CHAPTER 6

Horse Shows

For several years, our local veterinary association had been providing veterinary oversight at a local charity horse show. When I say oversight, I mean we would check to make sure the horses had the proper health papers and other tasks that did not involve medical treatment of the horse. If for some reason a horse needed medical or surgical treatment, the owner either called his usual veterinarian or paid the veterinarian who was on the premises at the time.

My volunteer time fell on Sunday evening. I loaded my wife and our three children in the cab of my pickup practice truck, and we drove the thirty miles to the fairgrounds where the show was held, hoping for a pleasant evening. I didn't anticipate having to do much other than check health papers, but I was in for a surprise.

When I drove onto the fairgrounds and parked my truck, I immediately had three men dressed in business suits at the driver's side window. I recognized one of them as a Dr. Dickerson, who was employed by the U. S. Department of Agriculture as a veterinarian. I had no idea who the other two men might be.

However, I soon learned when Dr. Dickerson handed me a piece of paper and said, "These are new regulations regarding the 'soring' of horses," and indicating the regulations referred to Tennessee Walking Horses. It turned out that the regulations in the form of the U. S.

Horse Protection Act of 1970 had been passed by the U. S. Congress earlier in the year, but for some unknown reason veterinarians hadn't been informed. At least, I hadn't received the new regulations.

I was also told by the feds that I was to examine the lower front legs of each Tennessee walking horse to make sure there was no evidence of soring. Dr. Dickenson then informed me that he and the two other federal veterinarians would be at the gate of the show ring to check the horses on their way out to ensure that I had not allowed an illegal horse to be shown. I thought to myself, "If they think I'm not capable of doing the job right, they should be in the ring doing the initial exam." However, once I started the exams of the horses among the hostile owners and riders, I knew why they were staying outside.

The Horse Protection Act ruled soring an abusive and illegal practice. Soring involves the use of chemical and other caustic agents being applied to the lower forelegs, causing burning or blistering of the skin. The pain resulting from the damage to the skin causes the horse to lift its forelegs higher when moving, because they are shown with pieces of small chain around the lower leg. These pieces of chain bat against the skin as the horse lifts and lowers its feet.

Since the horse is lifting its forefeet higher, it also brings it rear feet further under the body, resulting in a movement known as the "big lick." This gait was first developed in the 1940's and '50's and is a real crowd pleaser. The more the judges rewarded the horses showing the "big lick" gait, the more soring was done.

I had only one client who owned and showed Tennessee Walking Horses and he was too laid back to injure a horse so he could win a ribbon or trophy. I had never seen any evidence of soring by this man. In fact, until I was approached by the federal veterinarians at the show, I don't believe I had ever heard of the practice. For certain, no one had mentioned soring in our veterinary curriculum.

I was probably overly cautious when I examined the horses. I believe that, out of the first eight horses, I eliminated two or three. The first horse that I denied the opportunity to be shown exhibited scars on the front of the lower leg. On the front of the second horse's lower foreleg, I saw blood seeping through the skin. When I told the owner she could not show the horse, she accused me of deliberately scratching the horse's skin with my fingernails. Have you ever tried to scratch a horse's hide deep enough to make it bleed, using only your fingernail?

I later learned the young lady was the Secretary of the Illinois Tennessee Walking Horse Association.

In addition to the nasty comments I was receiving from the people handling the horses, I was being harassed by other persons who were standing outside the fence enclosing the area where I was examining the horses.

One woman outside the fence kept up a running commentary on me, my examination of the horses and any other thing she could think of. Finally, I said to her, "If you're unhappy with what is going on, I suggest you contact your congressman. They wrote the bill requiring the examination."

She said, "Oh, I don't care. I own Quarter Horses."

The last horse brought to me to be examined was a beautiful bay and his handler was a BIG young man -- about six feet four inches tall and weighing around 240 pounds. The horse's name was Roy Rogers.

When I arose from kneeling after examining the horse's lower limb, I showed the young man the greasy compound on my fingers and said, "I can't allow this horse to show."

The owner immediately showed me a small piece of paper on which was written, *"This horse is being treated with sulfathiazole and aquafor"* and which was allegedly signed by a veterinarian. The sulfathiazole was an antibacterial powder suspended in the ointment aquafor for easier application to wounds on the lower forelegs. After I explained to the young man that the note did not say why the horse needed to have the compound applied, he emphatically said, "Let him show!"

I was starting to be concerned for my health because my slight frame of five feet eight inches and 140 pounds was no match for this young giant. My nine year old son, Jimmy, was sitting on top of the bed of my practice truck, and the tailgate of the truck was down. On the tailgate was my twitch, an instrument for settling an agitated horse.

A horse twitch is piece of wood about 18 inches long with a hole drilled in one end. A piece of rope or chain long enough for the upper lip of a horse to be placed through it runs through the hole. The upper lip of the horse is held in the left hand while the chain or rope loop of the twitch is slipped over the lip. The handle of the twitch is then turned clockwise until the loop of chain or rope is snug around the upper lip. The purpose of the twitch is not to harm the horse, but only to take his attention away from what is being done. The holder of the horse usually is holding on to a rope attached to the halter with his right hand and holding the twitch with his left. The tightening and loosening of the loop on the lip by the handler keeps the horse's attention on the twitch, rather than on what is being done to him.

About that time, the young handler of the horse pushed his body up against mine, and viciously said, "I said, let him show!!" I was about ready to reach for my twitch to help protect myself when a policeman stepped between us and ushered the young man away.

I placed my equipment in my truck, and as Jimmy and I drove through the gate where the federal veterinarians were standing, Dr. Dickenson asked, "Did you throw that Roy Rogers horse out of the show?" When I nodded yes, he said, "He's been thrown out of every show they've tried to enter him in this year."

We then parked our truck in the parking lot and went to the stands to watch the rest of the horse show with my wife and other two children.

I was still apprehensive that Roy Rogers' owner would try to cause me and my family some harm when we left the fairgrounds. Other people must have had the same feeling, because we had a police escort out to the highway which was about a mile away.

I was in my office at about seven o'clock the next morning when the phone rang. When I answered, a voice on the other end of the line said, "This is Dickerson, I'm glad you're alive." I asked, "What do you mean?" He replied, "We heard there was a shooting in Kankakee last night, and we hoped it wasn't you." And that was the explanation for why the three federal veterinarians wanted me to examine the horses and make the decision whether or not they would be allowed to show. So much for their intestinal fortitude.

I was scheduled to act as the veterinarian for the Iroquois County Fair in about three weeks, but after my stint at the charity horse show I was not sure I wanted to do any more horse shows. I knew there was a Tennessee Walking Horse Class at the fair.

The chairman of the horse show at our fair was one of my clients, so I knew she would help me as much as possible.

In order to keep the kibitzers from interfering with the examination procedures prior to the horse show, I requested that at the time of the exams only the horse, a horse handler or rider, the show steward and I be allowed in the examination area. I also requested that the exam area be located away from the show arena.

With no extra persons to interfere and no unnecessary conversation, the examinations were conducted quickly and in an easy manner. Horses that had not been allowed at the previous show were cleared by me to enter the show. Perhaps this was because the owners had cleared up any problems the horses had exhibited earlier, or perhaps because I was not under the scrutiny of the federal agents (they did not show up for this show) and was not quite as strict.

I did learn, however, that the young lady who had accused me of scratching the foreleg of her horse with my fingernail withdrew her entry when she learned I would be the veterinarian at the show.

About two weeks later I received a phone call on a Sunday afternoon on my home phone. When I answered, the caller asked if I were Dr. Day. When I acknowledged that I was, he said, "I hear you run a pretty good horse show."

My reply was, "I think the answer to that would depend on who you ask."

He went on to explain that he was the chairman of a horse show to be held in Champaign, Illinois, (sixty-five miles away) three weeks hence, and he inquired if I would be interested in acting as the show veterinarian.

I said, "I doubt if you pay enough money to get me come that far for a horse show."

He answered, "Last year we paid 300 dollars and the vet only came three miles."

This was 1970, and 300 dollars was a lot of money, but I had had enough horse shows for the year, so I graciously declined.

CHAPTER **7**

Dangerous Bites

During my third year in veterinary school, anti-rabies vaccinations were offered to all the members of our class. However, I was allergic to the vaccine, and thus did not receive it. Three years later, I was sorry I had not been vaccinated.

It was November, and farmers had turned their cows into the recently harvested cornfields to glean the corn that the harvesting machines had missed. The cows wandered through the fields eating the kernels off the ears of corn still on the downed stalks.

I received a phone call around seven o'clock in the evening about a cow that was acting strangely out in the cornfield. When I arrived, the cow was lying down in the normal position and was alert, that is, her ears were up and her eyes were bright. I checked her temperature and it was normal.

I decided the cow had probably overeaten on corn, so I dosed her with mineral oil by using a stomach tube and pump. All the while I was treating her, a little voice in the back of my mind kept asking "Rabies?", "Rabies?" However, I was wearing gloves when I passed the stomach tube.

After I removed the stomach tube, I placed it and the pump in a pail of water and disinfectant. Then, we offered the cow a bucket of water, and she readily drank it. It is said that animals with rabies suffer from hydrophobia, a fear of water. When she drank the water, I thought, "She doesn't have rabies." I took my gloves off before removing the lariat from around her neck. Placing my gear in the trunk of the car, I told the farmer I would return at nine o'clock the following morning.

When I arrived at the farm the next morning, the cow was lying down in a normal position. However, when I approached her she readily arose. She walked a few feet, let out a strange bellow, and immediately dropped to the ground…. telltale signs of a cow that has rabies.

Since there was no treatment I could administer, I told the farmer she would probably die within twenty-four hours, and instructed him to phone me immediately so I could take her head to the University of Illinois for a positive diagnosis of rabies. The pathologists at the laboratory would examine her brain for evidence of rabies.

The farmer phoned the next morning to report that the cow had died during the night. After I finished the morning farm visits that I had scheduled, I drove to the farm, removed the head from the cow and started for the U of I. The farmer decided he would ride with me.

Soon after we had delivered the head to the pathology lab and started for home, it began to rain.

Then the rain turned to sleet, and the roads became slick. In fact, on the way home, we watched as a semi-truck and trailer slid into the ditch just ahead of us. Fortunately, the driver wasn't injured. Then darkness set in, and that made driving even more hazardous. All in all, a trip that should have taken three and a half hours turned into a five and a half hour ordeal.

When I saw the look on Mary Jane's face as I walked in the door, I knew the lab had phoned, and the news wasn't good. The phone call was confirmation that the cow was indeed rabid. This meant that I probably would need to take the thirteen subcutaneous injections of anti-rabies vaccine.

The following morning I phoned our family physician and made an appointment to see him. After hearing my story about the rabid cow, he thought it advisable for me to receive the rabies vaccine in case I had been exposed.

I received the first injection from the doctor. He gently pinched a fold of skin on my abdomen and injected the vaccine between the skin and muscle. I was then instructed to return to his office the following day and on subsequent days for twelve more injections.

The first five injections were made in a line across my abdomen parallel to the floor.

The next four injections were made down the left side of my abdomen from the last injection down toward my groin, and the last four injections were made on the right side from the groin up to the first injection.

After the doctor gave the first injection of the vaccine, I was to be injected by nurses. The nurse who gave me the next three vaccinations was just as meticulous as the doctor in making sure she gave the vaccine subcutaneously.

However, the fifth day I was greeted by a different nurse who disdained picking up the skin to make sure the injection was given subcutaneously. From a position about six inches from my body she jabbed the needle into my side. It felt to me like she had poked the needle into one of my ribs. I have a pretty high threshold for pain, but the shock of that injection brought tears to my eyes.

As I exited through the waiting room, an acquaintance who was sitting there said, "What happened to you, Doc? Your face has turned green."

As I recall, I didn't answer, just kept walking.

The nurse's injection technique was a little better the next day... at least she didn't hit a rib.

The vaccine used to prevent rabies after exposure was developed by Louis Pasteur, who used it successfully, in 1885, on a young boy badly mauled by a rabid dog.

I had always heard how painful the vaccine injections were. I would have to say that, other than the one injection, the shots themselves did not cause me that much pain.

However, the vaccine was not very pure and resulted in an enlargement of both my axillary and inguinal lymph nodes which filtered the impurities from the vaccine. In addition, the skin of my abdomen became thickened and inflamed. The combination of enlarged lymph nodes and inflamed, thickened abdominal skin made it very uncomfortable as I drove on my farm visits each day.

※ ※ ※

Probably more memorable than the case involving the cow and me, was the case involving a two year-old boy and a rabid bat.

The parents had been awakened at two o'clock in the morning by screams coming from the room of their young son.

When the father went into his son's room in response to the screams, he found a bat latched onto the skin between the thumb and forefinger of the little boy's hand.

The father quickly went to the kitchen and got a glass jar with a screw on lid, carried it back to the bedroom and knocked the bat into the jar and replaced the lid. He then made holes in the lid so the bat could have fresh air, which wasn't really necessary because I would euthanize the bat before sending it to the lab anyway.

The family had used the fireplace in the living room the previous evening and had neglected to close the damper in the chimney. The open chimney provided the entrance for the bat into the house.

The father brought the glass jar containing the bat to my office the next morning. In that jar was one angry bat. It kept opening and closing its mouth and, although the bat dentition is similar to humans, I believe that mouth was the ugliest I have ever seen.

Now I was in a quandary. I had to figure out a way to get the bat euthanized without letting it bite me.

After contemplating the problem for a while, I suddenly had an inspiration.

I kept on hand a number of seal-a-meal bags and the tool to seal them. This was because I often sold sodium sulfathiazole to farmers to dissolve in the drinking water of animals affected with pneumonia.

My plan was to remove the lid from the jar and, providing the bat did not escape, slip the bag over the mouth of the jar. Then, I intended to turn the jar upside down and shake the bat into the bag. Following that procedure, I would seal the bag

Eureka!! My plan worked. I now had a live bat sealed in a plastic bag.

I then drew two cubic centimeters of euthanasia solution into a small syringe and needle and injected the solution through the plastic bag into the abdominal cavity of the bat. Within a few minutes, the bat had absorbed the solution through the peritoneal lining of the body cavity and was dead.

The bat was packed in a box and sent to a U.S. Department of Agriculture laboratory in Peoria, Illinois. Forty eight hours later, I had my answer. The bat was positive for rabies.

Fortunately for the little boy, rabies vaccination procedures had improved considerably and he had to receive only three doses of vaccine and one dose of hyper immune serum.

❧❧❧

Another case of bat rabies occurred when a client found one of her cats playing with a bat during the night. The bat had come in through an open window and the cat had it on the floor and was using it as a toy. The lady managed to capture the bat and bring it to me the next morning. Unfortunately, she could not recall which of her twelve house cats was playing with the bat.

Results of the test for rabies on the bat by the lab were positive.

I phoned the Illinois Department of Agriculture at Springfield for advice on how to handle the situation. I was told by the powers that be that she must either euthanize all twelve cats, or keep them quarantined in individual cages for six months. Naturally, the owner opted to quarantine the cats.

At the end of the six month period, all cats were healthy. I then vaccinated them against rabies with a vaccine that would keep them safe for three years.

　　　　　　　　　　◢◢◢◣

Another case of rabies exposure that was quite interesting involved a cat with a litter of kittens and a skunk.

A cat owner brought in a mother and one baby kitten for rabies observation, telling me that earlier in the week he had found a skunk in with the cat and kittens. Since that time, five of the six kittens had died.

It was about eight a. m. when the cat and kitten were presented at my office. The kitten was nursing at the time. At noon, the kitten was dead.

As usual in such a case, I immediately sent the body of the kitten to the laboratory for rabies examination. The next day, I was informed that the kitten had died of rabies.

I immediately phoned the owner and informed him of the kitten's death and the cause. I also suggested that I euthanize the mother cat since she had obviously been exposed to rabies as well, and he agreed.

He was also quite concerned because his daughter held a pajama party with some of her friends the previous weekend, and the girls had been holding the kittens up to their faces.

I suggested that he phone his doctor and tell him everything about the sleepover and the girls' playing with the kittens.

Apparently the father did as I suggested, because I later heard that all the girls had undergone vaccination against rabies.

In the case of the rabid cow, I would assume that she had most likely been bitten by a rabid fox, although a rabid skunk was a possibility. Both rabid foxes and skunks had been found in our county at that time.

And the two cases of bat rabies are cut and dried because the rabid bats were found with the little boy and the cat.

However, I have always been perplexed by the kittens. Had the rabies virus been transferred by bite, there should have been evidence of wounds on the kitten's body.

Since there were no wounds, I have to surmise that the kittens inhaled the virus through the skunks expired air, or through breathing saliva. It is a known fact that rabies can be acquired by inhalation.

CHAPTER **8**

Bad Air

A young swine farmer came into my office one cold winter day and presented me with the tag off of an electric motor that ran a ventilation fan.

"How many cubic feet of air will that motor move per minute?" he asked.

"I'm no ventilation engineer, but I would assume the amount would be dependent on the size of the fan blades and how fast the blades were turning," I replied. "Why do you ask?"

"I have water dripping from the ceiling of my farrowing house, and the county ag adviser told me I'm not moving enough air into the building," he replied.

Danny had recently purchased some buildings that had been used for feeding turkeys to be slaughtered. I had only been in the building once or twice, so I had to stop and think about the layout.

I did remember that the building was equipped with roof vents which could be opened or closed as the owner chose. The purpose of these vents was to allow warm air to be brought into the building in cold weather.

"Are your roof vents open or closed?" I asked. "Closed!" he emphatically replied, "I don't want to get snow in the attic of the building."

"So you're bringing air directly from the outside into a heated building?" I asked.

"Yes."

"What is the temperature outside right now?" I asked him. "And what is the temperature inside the building?"

"Five degrees outside and sixty degrees inside," he answered.

"What happens when cold, damp air and warm air meet?" I asked.

"You get condensation," he said.

"Right," I replied, "but if you open your roof vents and bring partially warmed air into a heated building, you will not have water dripping from the ceiling."

"I'll let you know tomorrow how it works," he said as he walked out the door.

The next morning I received a call from Danny, "Thanks, Doc. Everything's fine in the farrowing house."

ﭮﭮﭮﭮ

"Doc, I need some antibiotics for my sows in the farrowing house because they are all running a fever and most aren't eating," said Louie Langan over the telephone. "Mix me up sonething, and I'll be in to pick it up."

Louie had built a new farrowing house a couple of years ago, and he was quite proud of it. The construction was nice, but it was labor intensive. His sows were in elevated farrowing crates, and this meant a lot of work cleaning the manure out from under the crates and disposing of it each day.

I knew about this because I owned a farrowing operation with sows in elevated crates. The difference was that we could push the manure down to a tile in the foundation of the farrowing house and then wash it into an outside pit.

Louie had to carry manure from his sows outside and pile it.

Later, he would load it on a manure spreader and apply it to his fields.

Two or three days later, Louie phoned again and wanted more antibiotics for his sows.

"Aren't your sows any better, Louie?" I asked him. "Some are," he replied.

I mixed up the antibiotics he wanted, and he came in to get them when I was out of the office.

Two days later, Louie called again and wanted more antibiotics. I told him, "Louie, I think I should come down and look at your sows."

He agreed.

I didn't have any immediate appointments so I got in my practice truck and drove the fifteen or so miles to Louie's farm.

When I walked into the farrowing house, I immediately smelled the odor of hogs, which is natural in a hog house. However, this was the stale odor of hogs -- meaning that the ventilation system either wasn't working properly, or wasn't properly designed to handle the air in this particular building. The smell of ammonia also assailed my nose.

Since the system had worked fine up until now, I suspected that Louie had more sows and pigs in the house than the ventilation system was designed for.

"Louie, how many sows and litters was this house designed to hold?" I asked. He responded, "Twelve."

"How many sows are in the house at this time?" I questioned.

"Sixteen."

"I believe that you are overtaxing your ventilation system. Breathing of stale air will cause a sow to run a temperature, and when they run a temperature, they won't eat."

I checked the temperature of two or three sows, and the readings were the same for all of them -- 103 degrees. Normal would have been 100 to 101 degrees Fahrenheit.

Since none of the three sows were nursing pigs, I suggested that we take them out of the crates and put them in the loafing shed which would be cooler than the farrowing house. I instructed Louie to check their temperatures at three p.m., the time at which the temperatures would be the highest for the day. I also asked him to call me with his findings.

At three fifteen that afternoon, my phone rang.

It was Louie. "Hey, Doc, the sows are all eating, so I didn't check their temps."

"Louie, your sows weren't sick with a disease. The antibiotics you gave them did no good. They weren't eating and were carrying a temperature because they were breathing bad air. You now have to make a decision."

"Do you want to raise fewer pigs, or do you want to spend money and improve your ventilation system to handle more sows and pigs? It's up to you."

Situations like this happened often. In order to save money on veterinary services, farmers would make their own diagnoses and come to me to buy medicines to treat the diseases they believed the animals were suffering from.

Louie spent about two hundred dollars with me on antibiotics which the sows didn't need. If he had called me to come out in the first place, all he would have had invested was the fee for a farm visit.

Through the years, I had developed a sense of smell that told me when a hog confinement building was not properly ventilated. Sometimes, it wasn't the ventilation system at all. Many of these buildings had slatted floors with a pit for collecting the liquid waste from the animals. The rule of thumb was that the level of the manure should not be closer to the slats than eighteen inches. There was a little leeway, but if the level of the manure rose close enough to the slats that the animals were inhaling ammonia, respiratory diseases occurred.

Hog and cattle confinement buildings were not the only buildings where improper ventilations could cause problems.

♪♪♪

I recall an occasion when I was called to a horse farm to see a standardbred race horse that wasn't eating or, "off his feed," as they say.

When I arrived, I found a gelding in a corner stall of a building that housed probably sixty horses. There were four rows of box stalls and two alleyways running between each two rows of stalls.

When I examined the horse, I found his respirations to be rapid, although the lungs were clear. His temperature was elevated about two degrees. Otherwise, he was alert and his eyes were bright.

"Do you have an empty stall toward the middle of this row of box stalls?" I asked the owner.

"Sure," he replied.

I suggested that we move the horse to that stall and watch him for about three or four hours.

It was an exceptionally warm day in May, and the air was quite still. My thought was that the horse, in that corner stall, was overheated from not receiving enough air.

When I returned to the farm at two p. m., the horse's temperature was normal, his respirations were normal, and he had eaten all his ground feed.

❧❧❧❧

I was at a regional veterinary meeting one time, and one of the speakers was a friend of mine. He related that he had been confronted with a problem in a swine farrowing house where the baby pigs were dying of pneumonia while still nursing the sow.

He determined that the pneumonia was caused by a lack of ventilation, so he suggested the farmer add more windows and fans to the house. Apparently, this solved the problem.

After the meeting I asked my friend the distance between the manure in the pit and the slats in the floor. He answered, "about three inches."

I suggested he might have solved the problem in a less expensive manner if he had told the farmer to empty the pit.

❧❧❧❧

At one time, I owned nearly seventy-five sows. Each month, twelve of those sows gave birth to a litter of pigs. When those pigs reached thirty-five to forty pounds in weight, we sold them to farmers who grew and fattened them for market.

I sold one group of fifty pigs to a local farmer, whom I knew to be a griper and complainer and who was never satisfied with anything.

About two weeks later he came to my office to tell me those pigs were sick. Since the pigs were perfectly healthy when I sold them to him, I knew there had to be a problem on his farm. I agreed, at no cost to him, to go out to his farm to examine the pigs.

I found pigs that were coughing, some in the early stages of pneumonia. These pigs were on slatted floors over a pit in a totally enclosed ventilated building. The manure was up to within two inches of the floor.

I explained to the farmer that the pigs were breathing ammonia fumes from the top of the manure and the fumes were irritating the lungs. To cure the sick pigs, he needed to lower the level in the manure pit by pumping it out and spreading it on his fields.

Although I knew I had sold him healthy pigs, I gave him some sulfa powder to put in the water for the pigs. I also vowed I would never sell pigs to him again.

CHAPTER 9

Tales of Dogs

As the lady placed the young dog on the table, she said, "I don't know why, but my puppy is bleeding from the rear end."

I lifted the dog's tail and immediately saw the enlarged vulva with the blood oozing out from between the lips.

"Your dog is in heat, ma'am," I said.

"He can't be… he's a male."

"No, she's a female."

"The people who gave him to us said he's a male."

"I'm sorry but the people who gave the puppy to you were wrong. She's a female and she is in heat."

Grabbing the dog and hugging her tightly to her breast, the lady almost ran from my exam room, through the waiting room, and out the front door.

I didn't see the dog again for nearly twelve years when she developed a heart condition. I don't know where she had been taking her or why she came back to me. I do know that we kept the dog alive until she was seventeen years old.

꙰꙰꙰

Another veterinarian had been treating an English bulldog for a chronic skin condition under the tail off and on for two years. As the owner told the story, after the dog had been on medication (probably a cortisone derivative, although the owner claimed not to know) for two weeks, the problem would clear up for about a month. Then the condition would recur, and the attending veterinarian would prescribe the same medication.

On that particular day I had a younger veterinarian, Dr. Rodger Allhands, working with me and, as I was talking to the owner, he was examining the tail. He said, "Look at this, the tail is fused, I can't move it."

And as they say, therein lay the problem. Since the tail lay flat to the body, and couldn't be moved or wagged, moisture would collect and cause the skin to be inflamed. Anti-inflammatory drugs would work for a while, but once they were stopped, the condition would recur.

The solution to the problem was to amputate the tail as high up as feasible so the area would stay dry. Moist dermatitis would then not recur.

The next day we amputated the tail at the base, and when we removed the sutures a week later the dog was healed, never to itch again.

><><><

It had been a month since I had diagnosed heart failure in the mixed Terrier female owned by Mr. Delson. The charges for the office visit and the thirty diuretic tablets I dispensed had totaled twenty six dollars.

As he entered the door, I assumed he had come for a refill on Trixie's prescription. When I greeted him, instead of asking for a refill, he asked, "Will you write me a prescription for Trixie's medicine so I can get it through AARP?"

"No sir," I replied. "I don't believe AARP enrolls dogs, and if they do, she's not old enough." After all, it was costing him the large sum of ten cents a day to keep his aged dog alive and I was getting rich on the profits.

"I would be happy to write a prescription for you to purchase Trixie's pills at any of the pharmacies in town."

"They'd probably just rip me off like you're doing. Okay, go ahead and refill the prescription," he grouchily said.

When I handed him the bottle of pills, he gave me the three dollars, turned and walked out the door and I never saw him again.

I don't know if the dog died, if he just quit giving Trixie her pills, or if he found someone to sell him the pills for less than ten cents each.

᠌᠍᠎᠏

"Doctor, I don't know what I have here," said the lady as she placed the Boston terrier on the examination table.

To be frank, I didn't know what she had either. It was the first hermaphrodite puppy I had ever seen.

There was a small hole, not much bigger in diameter than the lead in a pencil, about half way down in the perineal area. There was no vulva.

The penile sheath looked like someone had sliced it down the middle and spread the sides. Dangling from the penile sheath, about where the penis should have been, was a flat, wrinkled, pink, wavy piece of tissue masquerading as a penis.

"Can you do anything for this puppy, Doctor?" asked the lady.

"Since the puppy is urinating through the small hole in back between the legs, there is no need to try to preserve the penis. So, what I recommend is amputating the non- functional penis and closing up the penile sheath. There are no testicles in evidence, so the puppy must have a uterus and ovaries. However, she can never get bred, because no dog could penetrate that small opening where she urinates," I explained to the lady.

By amputating the penis and trimming back the edges of the penile sheath and suturing them together, we gave the puppy a fairly smooth abdomen.

My only concern was that the puppy might suffer from urine burns around the small opening where she urinated.

I was not able to follow up on this puppy as it grew older because the owners moved away shortly after I performed the surgery.

ッッッ

There was an elderly lady who insisted her dog was infested with fleas. It was a terrier, a short haired dog, so it was easy to part the hair and see right down to the skin, and I could find no fleas. I sprayed the dog with flea spray, and no dead fleas dropped off. There were no black specks of flea dirt (manure) in front of the tail.

I said to the elderly man who had brought the dog in for me to examine, "See if that satisfies her, Louie. If not, bring the dog back in a week."

Six days later, Louie showed up with the dog. I went over the dog with a fine toothed comb and saw no fleas or flea dirt (manure).

"I don't know what to tell you, Louie, but I do not see any fleas. I don't understand how the owner continues to see them."

Louie, who was the lady's neighbor and friend said, "Don't let it bother you, Doc. She sees little green men running around the house, too."

ッッッ

I had been called to the farm of a horse client who owned Saddlebreds to perform two pregnancy exams. I arrived at the farm before my scheduled appointment and, seeing no one outside, knocked on the kitchen door.

I was greeted with a "C'mon in, Doc, and have a cup of coffee." They had almost finished their coffee, and when they did I was told, "Take your time while we get the horses in the barn. When you've finished your coffee, come out to the barn."

They owned a big male Weimaraner dog and he stayed in the kitchen with me.

When I finished my coffee, I set the cup down on the table and started to rise from the chair. "Grrr" was the sound I heard. I saw the bared teeth.

After sitting there a while longer, I started to rise again. Again, "Grrr," and more bared teeth.

Four times I tried to rise from the chair to go to the barn, and four times the dog growled. I do believe he would have bitten me if I had gotten all the way out of the chair.

I was still sitting in the chair when the door opened, and in walked Carolyn, one of the horse owners. "What have you been doing in here?" she asked.

"Sitting. The dog won't let me out of the chair."

♩♩♩♩

Our neighbors owned an eleven year-old mixed breed female dog. I had noticed that, for several weeks, she had walked around with her rear legs spread as if she were attempting to urinate. Once, as I got closer to her, I could see the urine dripping from her vulva.

Finally, the owners brought her to my office for an examination. After we had placed her on the examination table, I placed a hand on either side of her abdomen and what I felt was a rock nearly as big as a softball. The "rock" was more oval in shape, however.

I did not yet own an x-ray machine, so I explained to the owner that I would need to do exploratory surgery to determine the problem. He agreed, and we kept the dog for surgery the following day.

The next morning, after prepping the dog for surgery in the usual manner, I incised her abdominal tissues and then brought the urinary bladder outside the body before cutting into it. The bladder was distended to its fullest size and was packed with urinary calculi (bladder stones). The dog had been dripping urine because there was no room in the bladder for urine to be stored…the urine ran directly from the kidneys, and through the bladder and urethra.

There were a total of thirteen stones weighing thirteen and three quarter ounces. The smallest stone weighed a half ounce and the largest three ounces.

And, as it is said, the dog went on to make an uneventful recovery. She lived to be fifteen years old.

ᗞᗞᗞ

"Doctor, there's something seriously wrong with my dog," a breathless voice said on the other end of the phone line.

"What do you mean?" I asked.

"She's just lying on the floor, not breathing."

"What color are her gums?"

"Purple."

"Does she have a heartbeat?" I asked the lady, who was a registered nurse.

"No."

"Mrs. Troup, I believe she is dead."

"I was turning somersaults on the living room floor and landed on her. Do you think I killed her?"

Mrs. Troup weighed more than two hundred pounds. The little dog weighed five.

"It's a good possibility."

ᗞᗞᗞ

Our son, Tom, was accompanying me on a call to treat a sick cow one Saturday morning. As we passed the farm of Ed Bagley, Tom pointed to the shoulder of the road and said, "Look, Dad, there's a dog lying there." I replied, "Yep, it looks like old Gunner was hit by a car."

About a half hour later, we were returning from treating the cow. Now it was my turn to say, "Look, Tom. Gunner has his head up…he isn't dead."

As I drove into Ed's driveway, I could see him near the hog house. We drove back there, and I got out of my truck and I asked, "Ed, do you know that Gunner was hit by a passing vehicle?"

"Yes, I'm getting ready to bury him now."

"Don't bother. He's alive and was holding his head up as we drove onto your property."

We all went out to Gunner, and I knelt down by him. I asked Ed to hold his head to keep him from biting me in case my examination caused him pain. Looking for possible fractures, I felt all his legs. I found a fracture of the left elbow.

Apparently, the blow by the auto or truck knocked Gunner unconscious but did not cause any internal injuries.

Ed brought Gunner to my hospital where I set and splinted the elbow.

Although Gunner was already showing some gray hairs among his red ones, he lived another five years.

↵↵↵↵

In addition to his Hereford cattle, "Heinie" Werner also owned a Border Collie dog.

One day, he brought the dog to my office because it had a large swelling on the right rear leg.

After determining that the swelling was a tumor, I suggested to "Heinie" that he leave the dog with me so I could remove the tumor.

Early the next morning, with Mary Jane assisting me, I removed the tumor. Although the surgery did not go as smoothly as I had hoped, I was pretty sure I had gotten the entire tumor.

About a week later, I removed the sutures and could feel no swelling where the tumor had been.

Two or three months passed before "Heinie" brought his dog back. When he did, Shep had an even larger swelling in the same area. Again, I kept the dog for surgery.

The first time I operated on the dog's leg, I made my incision on the outer side of the femoral area. Since that approach did not work, I decided to make my incision on the inside of the leg. Once again, I felt I had removed the entire tumor.

When "Heinie" came to get Shep the next day, he coughed and asked, "How much do I owe ju?"

I replied, "Nothing."

Then "Heinie" coughed and said, "Vy ju chipskate."

Another two months passed before "Heinie" returned with Shep. The tumor had returned.

I referred Shep to the Small Animal Clinic at the University Of Illinois College Of Veterinary Medicine. They removed the leg at the hip, and Shep got along very well on three legs. In fact, he lived longer than "Heinie."

⟫⟫⟫

It's amazing how adaptable a dog or cat can be.

When one of my farm clients brought in his terrier dog with two broken legs from being struck by a car, I anticipated the dog would be laid up in a stall in the barn for about three weeks.

The ends of the fractured femur of the dog's left rear leg were so badly displaced that after aligning them, I inserted an intramedullary pin the length of the bone. I then placed a splint made of aluminum rod on the leg. The other leg did not need pinning, so I merely splinted it.

About a week later, I was on the Jackson farm to treat a sick calf.

When I walked out of the barn, I saw the little dog chasing a cat. On his two front legs!! His splinted rear legs were pointed toward the sky.

⟫⟫⟫

At the age of six, I acquired my second pet...a puppy.

My father returned home from a farm sale one day with a mixed Chow puppy. I think he paid the grand sum of fifty cents for the little fella.

Chow became an excellent companion for me, following me nearly everywhere I went.

During the nice weather of fall and spring, he accompanied me to school and lay outside until lunch time when he would follow me home. Then back to school we went in the afternoon.

After school, he would trot behind me as I delivered newspapers on my bicycle.

Chow had one fault...he didn't like our neighbor's German Shepherd dogs.

When those dogs went past our house, Chow was going to fight with them. No matter that he had to jump over a picket fence three feet high. No matter that there might be two dogs to fight...he was going to fight them.

The only way to prevent fights between them was to keep Chow tied. I did part of the time, but not all the time.

❧❧❧

I answered the office phone about 7 a.m. one morning to hear a female voice on the other end say, "Doc, I needed you last night."

Recognizing the voice on the other end as the wife of a friend, I replied, "Really, what would your husband think about that?"

She said, "Oh, you. I needed you to see our dog, and you weren't home. We took him to another veterinarian and he died."

"What was wrong with your dog?"

"The tongue of a grain wagon fell on his head."

The tongue of a wagon is made of metal and is quite heavy.

"I'm sorry about your dog, but he probably would have died, even if I had seen him."

CHAPTER **10**

Inflated Cows

Members of the bovine species, both males and females, are sometimes affected with a condition called bloat. Bloat is a digestive disturbance characterized by an accumulation of gas in the first two compartments of the stomach of a ruminant animal.

In order to understand the cause, mechanism and effects of bloat, it is first necessary to know that a cow or bull has four compartments to her (or his) stomach. Many people believe that a bovine animal has four stomachs. Sheep and goats also have stomachs with four compartments. Camels' and llamas' stomachs have three compartments.

Cattle and sheep are known as ruminants; camels and llamas as camellids.

When cattle graze on grass or eat hay from a hay bunk or grain from a grain trough, the feed goes into the first compartment of the stomach, the rumen. From the rumen, the food moves into the reticulum where the bolus like cud is formed. Eructation or regurgitation or belching moves the cud back into the mouth, where the animal chews the food again. Chewing of the cud, along with the breakdown of the food by the bacteria in the stomach helps complete the digestion of the hay and grains taken in by the animal.

After chewing the cud, the animal swallows the food, and it enters the rumen again. Some of the food may go into the reticulum to be formed into new cuds, and some of it may move through the rumen to the next stomach compartment, the omasum.

The function of the omasum is to absorb water and some nutrients as the food passes through on its way to the true stomach, the abomasum.

The abomasum secretes protein and starch digesting enzymes to further break down the food that the rumen failed to digest. From the abomasum, the food moves into the small intestine for further digestion.

We don't need to go any further with our elementary introduction into the anatomy of a bovine digestive system, because the stomach is the site where bloat occurs. Actually, the rumen and the reticulum are the compartments where bloat occurs.

There are two types of bloat -- frothy and gaseous.

Frothy bloat occurs in animals grazing in pastures that have large amounts of legume plants, usually alfalfa, growing among the grasses. Animals are especially vulnerable to frothy bloat when they are allowed to graze in the early morning when the plants are wet with dew.

If animals suffering from frothy bloat are discovered in time, treatment is usually accomplished by passing a stomach tube through the mouth and into the rumen. Little gas will be released through the stomach tube, so it is necessary to pass medicine down the stomach tube to break up the bubbles and relieve the bloat.

Gaseous, or dry bloat, occurs when, for some reason, the animal is unable to belch to get the methane gas out of the rumen. Perhaps this is because the animal has overeaten or there is a mechanical blockage preventing the gas from leaving the rumen.

Whatever the cause of the bloat, the rumen will be distended, and the cow will look lopsided on the left side because that is where the rumen is located.

While I have treated a few cases of frothy bloat, many such cases were dead when the farmer found them on legume pastures covered with dew in the early morning.

One interesting case comes to mind when I think of dry or gaseous bloat.

Early one morning the doorbell rang at my home. Answering it, I was confronted by an elderly farmer dressed in bib overalls and a denim shirt, the usual attire for some older farmers.

When I opened the door this gentleman said in a strong German accent, "I haf a bloted cow." And then he coughed. When I asked as to the location of the cow, he said to follow him. And then he coughed.

I followed the man six or seven miles to his farm. When we arrived, I gathered my stomach tube, speculum, and stomach pump along with a jar of Carmilax laxative, and an empty pail. As I reached for my lariat, he said, "Ju won't need dat, I haf her tied up."

After handing the man (I still didn't know his name) my pail and asking him to get me about a gallon of lukewarm water, I headed toward the big red barn.

As I entered the barn, I could see a Hereford cow tied to the manger. I was impressed by the cleanliness of the barn. It was early fall, so the cows mostly stayed in the pasture, but the barn was clean and ready for bedding when the cows needed to come in from bad weather.

As the farmer entered the barn with the pail of water, I could hear him coughing. I poured the laxative powder into the warm water and stirred it well with my mouth speculum. Then I picked up my black neoprene stomach tube, inserted the end of it into the speculum and placed the speculum into the side of the cows mouth and past the molar teeth. After I had the speculum in the mouth properly so the cow could not chew on the stomach tube, I passed the stomach tube down the esophagus and into the rumen.

When I first inserted the mouth speculum into the cow's mouth, the farmer (I had now learned his name was Henry Werner) coughed and then said, "Ach, now I see how ju do hit, you uss a piz of gass pipe." There was a section of garden hose lying in the manger. Apparently his attempts at passing the garden hose down into the stomach had been thwarted by the cow because she kept chewing on the rubber hose.

Once the stomach tube reached the stomach, the malodorous methane gas came out in a rush, and the rumen returned to its normal size.

I finalized the treatment by pumping the gallon of water containing the laxative and rumen stimulant into the cow's stomach.

When I had finished cleaning my equipment and stowing it in the back of my station wagon, I wrote out a ticket for my services and handed it to the farmer.

"I come by tomorrow and pay ju," I was told by Mr. Werner. All the while we were treating the animal and since, he was coughing.

As I drove home, I was hoping he would pay me.

The next morning about eight o'clock the doorbell rang and there, true to his word, was Henry, or Heinie, Werner. As I let him in the door of my office, I heard him say, "Ju gott any schnapps?" I replied, "No sir, I haven't." His next words were, "Mein Gott, the next time I come pay my bill, ju better have schnapps."

A few days later, I was at another farm in the vicinity of the Werner farm, and I queried the neighbor about Henry Werner. First, I asked him about the bad cough, and he replied that Henry had inhaled poisonous gas during the First World War. My next question was, "Isn't the Department of Veterans Affairs doing anything to help him?"

"Hardly," came the reply, "he was in the German army."

Henry had emigrated to the United States during the 1930's.

☽☽☽

Arriving home from church services one Sunday about noon, we walked into the house to the sound of a ringing telephone. I answered it to hear the voice of Alva Snedeker telling me that he needed me right away to treat a bloated cow. Alva was an aging dairy farmer, who had sold his cows and quit milking once, but after a couple of years had bought some more cows and was back in business. When I asked him once why he started milking again, his reply was, "What else can you do at two-thirty in the morning?" He had risen so early for so many years, he could not sleep past that hour.

Arriving at the farm, I saw a big Holstein cow lying down in the cow lot with three of Alva's neighbors standing there with puzzled looks on their faces.

Alva met me at the gate to the barn lot and told me that his neighbor had stuck a knife into the cow's rumen, and the bloat had gone down, but the cow still could not rise to her feet.

I took one look at the cow and knew why she had bloated and why she could not get up. The barn lot sloped from the barn toward the road ditch, and the cow was lying with her back toward the road and her feet pointing toward the barn. A cow cannot rise when her feet are higher than her back.

I had my lariat in my hand, so I placed it around her neck, and placed a loop of it around her nose to make a halter. I tugged on the lariat, pulling her head around to the right side of her body while one of the men pushed on her shoulders.

Once we had her up on her sternum, she folded her front legs under her, raised her rear legs to a standing position and then stood on her forefeet.

Sticking a knife into a cow's rumen is the last resort when dealing with bloat. Usually, if an instrument is to be used to penetrate the rumen from the outside, it is a trocar and cannula. The trocar is a pointed instrument that fits through a metal tube.

The trocar and cannula are grasped in the hand and then rammed through the side of the cow into the rumen.

Usually, it is necessary to make a small incision in the skin before placing the instrument through the muscle The trocar is then removed and air escapes through the cannula. The cannula is about five-eighths of in inch in diameter, and doesn't do as much damage as a knife.

In the case of Alva's cow, however, the person who stuck the knife into the rumen did not remove it immediately, but left it in place. As the air came out and the pressure in the rumen lessened, the rumen began peristaltic movements, and this caused the knife to rip a gash in the rumen about six inches long.

Now that we had the cow standing on her feet it was necessary to get her in the barn with her head in a stanchion so that I could repair the damage done by the butcher knife.

After clipping the hair and cleansing and disinfecting the skin, I used a line block to deaden the skin and muscle before enlarging the incision in the skin. When the farmer jammed the knife through the skin, he made an incision about an inch and-a-half long. It was necessary for me to enlarge the skin incision so I had enough room to work while I was suturing the long tear in the rumen.

After finishing, I gave the cow an injection of antibiotics and instructed Alva to discard the milk for a few days because of the use of antibiotics.

A week later, I removed the sutures from the skin.

♪♪♪

Another example of what I call positional bloat occurred when I was called to treat a cow that was down in a cornfield.

When I arrived, I could see the cow lying out in the cornstalks about twenty rods from where I parked my truck.

As Harley, the farmer, and I walked out to the cow, I could see she was lying on her left side between two rows of corn stalks in a field that had been harvested recently.

Once again, I knew that the bloat was due to the fact that the cow's back was lower than her feet, and she could not roll up to a position where she could stand.

I placed my nose lead in her nasal septum and pulled on the rope to lift her head off the ground and around to the right while Harley pushed on the cow's shoulders. Once we had her sitting up, she immediately rose to her feet. Two or three belches expelled a lot of malodorous methane gas, and the swelling went down on her left side and she was normal again.

As the horned cow stood there with my nose lead still in her nose and the rope dangling on the ground, I knew we had a problem. Once someone tried to remove the nose lead, the cow would butt the person with her head and might do damage with her horns.

A nose lead is made like a pair of tongs with round and blunt ends that go in the cow's nose. The other ends of the instrument have holes so a rope may be inserted through them. When the lead is placed in the cow's nose and the rope is tightened, the blunt ends of the lead place pressure on the cow's nasal septum and help control her.

I wasn't brave enough to walk up to the cow and try to remove the lead from her nose, so I said, "Well, I guess I just lost a nose lead." A new one would only cost two or three dollars and I weighed the possibility of being hurt against the cost of a new nose lead. It was a no brainer. Besides, I knew the lead would drop out of the cow's nose as she walked across the cornfield. Harley might even see it when he plowed the next spring.

When Harley said, "I'll get it for you," I cautioned him, "Don't get hurt."

Harley slowly walked up to the cow, and as he reached for the nose lead, she butted him with her head, knocked him down, walked over him, and headed across the cornfield.

As I helped Harley to his feet, I asked, "Are you hurt?"

"Nah, I'm all right," he replied.

As we neared the house, Harley suddenly said, "I don't feel so good." "Will you take me to the doctor?"

I agreed to do that and asked, " Who is your doctor?"

When he replied, "Dr. Joe," I told him I would call my wife on the two-way radio and ask her to call his office.

I radioed Mary Jane, and while I waited she called Dr. Joe's office and relayed to me that she was told that I should take Harley to the hospital emergency room for examination.

After about forty minutes of waiting, I decided to go to the house to see what was keeping Harley. I was fearful that he actually was badly injured. As I approached the back door it opened and out stepped Harley dressed in a suit and tie. He had also taken the time to take a bath.

I deduced that there was not much wrong with Harley, but after examining him, the doctor hospitalized him for three days of observation.

⁂

One of my really good dairy clients phoned one day saying he needed for me to come out and treat a bloated cow.

There were some things that I considered emergencies and bloat was one of them so I made haste to get to his place.

When I arrived at the farm, Frank was waiting near the barn. I asked, "Where is the cow, Frank?" "She's in the barn lot, Doc." Simple question, simple answer.

As we walked into the barn lot, the cow was easily recognized because the left side of her abdominal area was quite puffy. "Let's get her into the barn, Frank," I said. As we were herding her, or following her, -- I don't know which, I noticed that her gait was not quite right. She seemed to be staggering a bit. The reason I suggested we might be following her instead of herding her is that when that barn door is open all the cows know where they should go.

When she was inside the barn, she immediately put her head into a stanchion and Frank closed it to keep her there.

For the non-farmers who might read this book, a stanchion is two pieces of metal or wood hinged at the bottom with a latch at the top. When closed, the stanchion is wider than the cow's neck and narrower than her head. The cow can lie down, eat hay or grain that is placed in front of her, but she can't get her head out of the stanchion.

I checked the cow's temperature, and it was slightly sub-normal. I could detect no movement of the rumen when I listened with my stethoscope.

"When's she due to have her calf?" I asked Frank.

"About two days," he replied, and then asked, "Why?"

"She's coming down with milk fever," I replied.

"Doc, you're full of it," Frank said.

"Maybe so," I laughingly answered, "but I'm going to give her a bottle of calcium gluconate anyway."

Returning to my practice vehicle, I retrieved a five hundred cc bottle of calcium gluconate, a two-inch, sixteen gauge needle, a rubber I.V. tube and a nose lead.

After placing the nose lead in the cow's nose and pulling her head up and to the right and wrapping the rope around the top pipe of the metal stanchions, I gave the rope to Frank to hold. I then inserted the needle into the cow's left jugular vein and tipped the bottle up so that the fluid would fill the I. V. tube and no air would go into the cows blood stream. I then connected the I. V. tube to the needle. It is necessary to administer the calcium gluconate slowly because if it is given too rapidly a heart block might be caused, and the cow would die.

After I had administered about half the calcium gluconate, the cow let out about two or three big belches, and the bloat was gone.

"Still think I'm full of it, Frank?" I asked.

"No, I think you were right, Doc, but it's hard to believe that a cow would bloat because she's coming down with milk fever."

Milk fever, or parturient paresis, is common in high producing dairy cows, especially Jerseys. The condition usually occurs two or three days after the cow delivers her calf, but sometimes precedes calving. It also occurs in beef cows occasionally.

Calcium is necessary for the transmission of nerve impulses over junctions in the nerves called synapses. I liken these junctions to draw bridges. When drawbridges are up, traffic cannot cross over the bridge. So, when the calcium level of the blood drops below a certain level, the drawbridges are up, and no impulses can cross.

In the case of Frank's cow, the lack of function of the nerves in the rumen caused the movement of the rumen walls to slow down, or even stop. This caused the buildup of gas and the bloated stomach.

When the level of calcium in the blood is restored to normal, the nerve function returns and rumen activity is restored.

᠈᠈᠈᠊

Occasionally, the farmer's diagnosis of bloat in a bovine animal turns out to be a totally different condition.

Once, I was called out on a Sunday afternoon to treat a bloated feedlot calf weighing about six hundred pounds. It was true that the left side of the calf's abdomen was bulging outward and upward, but for some reason it didn't look like bloat. In order to determine if it was gas in the rumen causing the bulging, after tying the calf to a manger with my lariat to restrain it, I inserted a large gauge three-inch needle through the skin and muscle and, I thought, into the rumen. No gas came out through the needle, but urine came out like a waterspout.

Steers being fattened for slaughter sometimes develop urinary stones or calculi.

Apparently, this calf had a stone lodged in its urinary bladder or the urethra just as it left the bladder and urine was leaking into the abdominal cavity. Had the stone been lodged in the calf's urethra, the urine would have been between the muscle of the abdomen and the skin. Believe me, there was a large amount of urine in the abdominal cavity.

I'm not sure why the surgery worked, but I performed a perineal urethrostomy and the calf began urinating through the urethra that I had exteriorized between the rear legs, and the steer survived.

⤙⤙⤙⤙

I had heard of Joss Fetterman having quite a cattle feeding operation and was hoping he would call for my services sometime. He did just that when he called me out to treat a bloated calf.

When I pulled onto the Fetterman premises, I saw the feedlot with cattle in it, but I also saw a pile of about six or eight dead calves weighing around 450 pounds each. Apparently, Joss had a new shipment of calves and they were having some problems with respiratory infection. I thought to myself, *'I wonder who's treating these calves.'*

About that time, Joss came out from behind the barn and yelled to me, "The calf's over here." When I saw the bloated calf, I was reminded of something I was told as a teenager when, for my summer employment, I worked at a stockyards for a feeder cattle dealer. The cattle dealer would purchase calves weighing from three hundred to six hundred pounds from ranchers in the west, mainly Nebraska, and resell them to local farmers for fattening.

The bloated steer that concerned Joss was a dwarf Hereford weighing about two hundred pounds with a bulging forehead, a lower jaw that protruded out past the upper jaw, a large abdomen and short legs.

This calf looked just like the one I had seen at the stockyards where I worked that summer. I asked one of the veteran workers about that calf, and he drawled, "Well, I'll tell you about that calf ....he's been dead for three days, and just doesn't know it."

The calf was dead when I went to work the next morning.

That's just how I felt about Joss' calf. He was dead and just didn't know it!

I treated Joss' calf for bloat, explained to him about dwarf calves and didn't offer him much hope for the calf's survival.

Dwarfism of genetic origin was common in the Hereford breed of cattle years ago but, I understand, has been nearly eliminated by genetic selection.

What bothered me more than the dwarf calf that I had just treated were the dead calves in the pile outside the cattle pen, so I asked Joss, "Who's treating your calves that are sick from shipping fever?"

"Oh, I treat them myself because you vets charge too much," he replied.

I must have missed something in my economics course, because I could have treated a lot of sick calves for what that pile of dead calves cost.

CHAPTER 11

Mrs. Moresby and Cheetah

It was nine o'clock on a Wednesday night, and our home telephone rang. Before I arose from my easy chair where I was sitting watching television, I knew who the caller was.

When I answered the phone, the voice of an elderly woman asked, "Doctor, do you think Cheetah could have inside hemorrhoids?"

This was not the first time she had asked that question of me. In fact, it had been posed to me on the phone nearly every Wednesday night for the past six months. It had also been asked each time Mrs. Moresby brought Cheetah to my office.

My response to the question was, "No, I don't think so, Mrs. Moresby." And then I always asked, "By the way, has Cheetah been spayed?"

"Oh, yes, Doctor," she replied. "She was already spayed when she was given to me."

I had my doubts that Cheetah had been spayed because her distended abdomen and enlarged, doughy vulva were signs of pyometra, also called pyometritis. Nor had I been able to see a scar on the midline of the abdomen. A scar would indicate that a spay had been performed. I was not about to call an elderly lady a liar though. If the condition worsened enough, pus would ooze from the vulva, and the dog would start showing signs of the illness. Her appetite would decrease; she would drastically increase her water consumption and her urine output and she would become lethargic.

Pyometra is a condition that occurs in older dogs that have gone through numerous heat cycles without having puppies. It is a combination of hormonal imbalance and infection, although often the pus is sterile. The condition may also occur in cats, humans and other animals.

The phone calls had continued nearly every Wednesday night for a year. I had figured out when the phone calls started that she really wasn't calling about Cheetah. She was calling because she was lonely and needed someone to talk to. I had no reservations about her calling me…someday I would become elderly and possibly lonely and I, too, might need someone to talk to.

Mrs. Moresby had a medical condition that required her to go to Chicago to see a doctor about once a month. When she did, she usually left Cheetah with a friend of hers, Mrs. Figgins.

On one occasion, Mrs. Moresby left Cheetah with Mrs. Figgins at eight o'clock on Sunday morning, and Mrs. Figgins called me at four p.m. and said she thought we should put Cheetah to sleep. I sort of hesitated, and Mrs. Figgins emphatically said, "Mrs. Moresby gave me permission to put her to sleep if I thought it necessary."

When I asked Mrs. Figgins why she wanted to euthanize Cheetah, she replied, "She's not eating." I then asked her how long Cheetah had been at her house and she replied, "About eight hours."

I said, "Mrs. Figgins, if Cheetah hasn't eaten by tomorrow at this time, call me and I will bring a euthanasia consent form to you. After you sign it, I will put Cheetah to sleep."

Apparently Cheetah started eating, or she didn't want to take responsibility for having Cheetah euthanized because Mrs. Figgins didn't phone me.

When Mrs. Moresby returned and retrieved Cheetah from Mrs. Figgins, she stopped at my office and, with tears in her eyes, thanked me for not euthanizing Cheetah.

I had known Mrs. Figgins for a while, so I was not surprised at her actions, because I had treated her dog more than once for a minor ailment at no charge to her. Otherwise, she would have insisted that I euthanize the dog. I think it was a ruse to get free veterinary service.

The next time Mrs. Moresby was scheduled to go to Chicago to see the doctor, she made arrangements to board Cheetah at my animal hospital. However, I had to agree to pick Cheetah up at her home and transport her to my hospital. Since I drove past her house on my way, it posed no problem for me to give Cheetah a ride. Mrs. Moresby always left early on a Sunday morning for her appointment the next day.

When I went for Cheetah, there was still a small amount of snow on the grass from the night before. The sidewalks were clear, and I paid no attention to the small coating of snow on the front edges of the steps leading up to her porch.

I had a small carrying cage made out of plywood that one of my clients had given me and I carried that up to the house. The porch was a high one, about four feet, with five steps leading up to it. As I climbed the steps, I could see Mrs. Moresby's friend waiting for me in the doorway.

The elderly lady opened the door, and I entered the kitchen. As I set the carrying cage on the floor, Cheetah walked toward me with her tail wagging. After placing Cheetah in the cage, I picked up the cage, went through the door and out onto the porch.

I started down the steps, forgetting about the snow the night before. The next thing I knew I was sitting on the ground in the grassy area about twelve feet from the porch, still holding the cage containing Cheetah. My chin hurt and it felt like I had a cut on my jaw. Apparently, there had been a small amount of snow on the first step and as I placed my foot on that spot, I went airborne.

Mrs. Moresby's very concerned friend asked, "Doctor, would you like to come in and rest?"

"No, thank you, Ma'am, I'm down here now, and I don't want to try it again."

Before long, my feeling about Cheetah having pyometra came

true. Mrs. Moresby brought her to my office in a depressed condition and said she was not eating. When she placed the dog on the table, I immediately checked her rear end and saw the profuse discharge of pus from her vulva.

"I'm sorry," I said to Mrs. Moresby, "but the people who gave you Cheetah either told you a falsehood or you misunderstood them. Cheetah has not been spayed, and she has an infection of her uterus. We need to spay her now or she will die."

We gave Cheetah some I.V. fluids and an antibiotic injection and kept her overnight preparatory to doing the surgery the next morning.

Cheetah was feeling better the next morning, so we prepped her and gave her more I.V. fluids while I was doing surgery.

The surgery was uneventful other than the fact I removed two uterine horns that looked as if someone had somehow shoved a baseball through her cervix and up each horn about half way. Each horn was about six or seven inches long. Cheetah was probably about a pound and a half lighter than when we started surgery. She really looked svelte.

She was awake but not standing when we left the hospital at six p.m. that day so we placed some water in the cage for her.

The next morning Cheetah was feeling much better and dove into the small amount of canned food we gave her.

When we removed the sutures a week later, Cheetah looked and acted about three years younger than she had for a long time.

She died about three years later at the estimated age of fifteen.

CHAPTER **12**

Things That Slither

I was in the midst of afternoon walk-in office hours when I saw an unkempt young woman enter and take a seat in the waiting room.

She waited quietly while I examined and treated my next three patients. Then, when I walked into the business area, stood behind the counter and nodded to her, she walked up to speak with me.

Her question to me was "Do parakeets attract copperhead snakes?"

"I'm sorry, I don't know," I answered. "Why do you ask?"

"Because a copperhead snake got in the bird cage and ate my parakeet, and now it can't get out of the cage."

I thought it much more likely that the snake she was dealing with was a bull snake, also called a milk snake. Bull snakes are known for inhabiting the areas around farm buildings where they eat mice. Farmers used to think the snakes sucked the teats of cows. Hence the name milk snake.

"Why don't you take the bird cage outside and open the little door and let the snake out?" I asked. "Then your problem will be solved."

"Oh, no it won't," she said, "I have another parakeet. "

I then said to her, "I don't think you need a veterinarian, I believe you need a carpenter."

"Why is that?" she asked.

"To plug up the holes in your house so the snakes can't get in," I answered.

Very seriously, she said, "You know, you might be right." She then turned and walked out the door.

ﻼﻼﻼ

"Doctor, I think my snake might have pneumonia," a female voice said on the other end of the telephone line.

I thought I recognized the voice, but to be sure to whom I was talking, I asked, "Who is this?"

"It's Sandy," she replied.

Sandy owned a Boa constrictor about six feet long. I don't believe the snake had a name, but if it did, I can't remember what it was.

"Why do you think your snake might have pneumonia?"

"The snake seems to be constipated, so I have been giving it mineral oil with an eye dropper. I'm afraid I might have gotten some of the oil into its lungs." She replied.

Sandy's husband worked at a hatchery, so the snake was fed a steady diet of baby chicks.

If there is anything I know less about than birds, it would have to be snakes.

However, I did know that snakes' lungs extend for a considerable distance along the length of the body.

"We could take x-rays of the snake's lungs to see if there is any indication of a problem," I told her.

In about a half an hour, Sandy and her snake were sitting in the waiting room of my animal hospital.

I informed Sandy that due to the snake's length, I would have to take several radiographs and she agreed.

I took the x-rays, developed them, and read them when they were still wet. I saw no problems concerning the lungs.

I walked up to the waiting room and informed Sandy of my findings.

About a week later, I received a phone call from an ecstatic

Sandy, who excitedly said, "My snake had a bowel movement -- on the window sill."

All I could say was, "Good for him!!"

⟩⟩⟩⟩

"We just killed a Massasauga rattlesnake," said an excited women over the telephone, "and we still have a baby snake."

I wanted to say, "No you didn't, we don't have Massasauga rattlesnakes around here," but instead I asked, "Did the snake have a rattle? " I knew that snakes sometimes shed their rattles.

"No," she replied.

"I believe you just killed a bull snake," I told her.

The markings on a bull snake are similar to those on a Massasauga snake. For an untrained person one snake might be mistaken for the other.

She continued to insist that the snake was a Massasauga, so I suggested she take the baby snake down to the University of Illinois to a herpetologist.

I never found out if, in fact, the snake was a Massasauga rattler.

Bull snakes are beneficial around farms. They eat mice in the barns and other farm buildings. Farmers once thought they sucked the milk cows, and they are sometimes called "milk snakes."

⟩⟩⟩⟩

Snakes and worms both slither, so I decided to include some worm stories along with the snake stories.

A well-dressed lady was sitting in my waiting room during walk-in office hours, and when it was her turn, I asked "What can I do for you, Mrs. Plantier?"

She replied, "I need some whipworm medicine."

I had done annual fecal exams on her two dogs a short time before, and both of them were negative.

"What makes you think you need whipworm medicine?" I asked.

"Because I have them," she replied.

"And how do you know that?" I asked.

"After I went to the bathroom, there was one floating in the water."

"How long was it, and what color was it?" I asked.

"It was black and about six inches long."

"Had anyone thrown a cricket in the stool before you went to the bathroom?"

"My husband did."

"You saw a horsehair worm, not a whipworm. Horsehair worms are long and black and spend part of their life cycle in the cricket. Whipworms are white and thin and about two to three inches long. When your husband threw the cricket into the stool water, the horsehair worm came out of the cricket."

Horsehair worms got their name from the fact that farmers often found them floating in the water tanks where horses drank. Since they resembled the hairs of a horse's mane, it was assumed the worms developed from hairs that had fallen into the water.

"My doctor sent the worm to a lab for identification. I'm supposed to hear from them in about a week."

A week later, the lady phoned to tell me the worm was indeed a horsehair worm.

When our granddaughter, Mindy, was a junior in high school, I took her and a friend to the U of I veterinary college to an open house as they both thought they were interested in becoming veterinarians. Mindy became a psychologist, the other girl a veterinarian.

As we wandered through the exhibit on internal parasites, I was particularly interested in one exhibit. In a jar of alcohol, a black worm floated. The jar was labeled as a heartworm. While heartworms are long…the females are longer than the males…they are white, not black. Someone had placed a horsehair worm in a jar and labelled it a heartworm. I knew who that someone was.

Later, I approached him at a veterinary meeting and chastised him for mislabeling the heartworm exhibit. His reply was that the heartworm turns black when placed in alcohol. I knew better because I had heartworms that had been in alcohol for thirty-five years, and they were still white. He had substituted a horsehair worm for a heartworm, hoping no one would notice.

❧❧❧❧

Another worm I saw quite often was the heartworm. No, I didn't see the adult heartworm…I saw microfilaria (baby heartworms) in the blood of a dog when I examined it under the microscope.

As a student at the University Of Illinois College Of Veterinary Medicine, I was told that heartworms were moving to the Midwest from the South. The heartworm microfilaria is spread from one dog to another by the bite of a mosquito. After biting a dog infected with heartworms, the mosquito bites a non-infected dog and injects the microscopic sized baby worm into that dog. Six months later, the dog is infested with adult heartworms.

The heartworms must have been moving fast because, in the first three months I was in Iroquois County, I diagnosed five cases of heartworm infestation. Four of the dogs were so severely infested that I referred them to the University of Illinois CVM for treatment. They probably had been infested the previous year. The fifth dog was a small terrier type dog. I was able to successfully treat her, and she lived to be fifteen years old.

In the early days of heartworm treatment, an arsenical compound was the drug of choice. Daily injections were given for fourteen days. Providing the dog's liver and kidneys had not been damaged by the heartworm infestation, the drug worked. If the dog's liver or kidneys were damaged, chances were the dog would die. It was very disheartening to have a dog survive for ten or twelve days, only to die the next day.

A few years after I began treating heartworms, the treatment regimen was reduced from thirteen to four days. The dogs seemed to tolerate the reduced treatment much better, and there were fewer deaths caused by the treatment.

After the adults were killed, oral treatment was given to kill the microfilaria. The microfilaria already in the dog's bloodstream would not develop into adult heartworms, but could be transmitted to other dogs by mosquitoes. The life cycle of the heartworm requires that the microfilaria be passed through a mosquito in order for it to be infective to other dogs.

Treatment of heartworms is much simpler today than it was in the beginning days of my practice.

Prevention of the disease is accomplished by the monthly dosing of one chewable tablet.

CHAPTER **13**

Heavy Metal

From the number of stories in this book about poisoning in animals, it would seem that poisoning occurs very often. That is not the case -- it's just that when poisoning does occur, it may be dramatic. It often takes some detective work to determine the type of poisoning and the source.

In order to spend time with our sons when they were young, and because I loved baseball, I managed Little League and Babe Ruth baseball teams for several years.

The games were played in late afternoon or early evening under the lights, and most of my clients knew where I would be in the evening. If they phoned me and no one answered, they knew where they could find me. Some clients would come to the ball park just to ask me a question about their animals, and some would come to ask me if I could come out to their farm the next day to see an animal.

At one game I was approached by a farmer I was acquainted with but for whom I had never treated any animals. He seemed to be in an agitated state when he called for me to come to the end of the dugout to talk with me. "Doc, I'm losing calves, and you've got to come out tonight to find out why." I resisted asking, "Why don't you call the veterinarian who usually does your farm work?" However, I already knew the answer.

He didn't make calls after four o'clock in the afternoon.

I assured the farmer that, since this was the first game of the evening, I would be at his place before darkness set in.

When I arrived at the farm, I could see a herd of about twenty Angus cows and several young calves in a pasture. The cattle also had access to the farmyard surrounding the abandoned house and other outbuildings.

I knew that this was a rented farm, because the previous tenant owned a herd of Hereford cows, and he had been a client before he retired and moved to town.

As I was gathering the equipment I would need to do an autopsy on the baby calf -- post mortem knife, rubber gloves, disinfectant, and plastic pail -- I surveyed the herd and the buildings on the farmstead.

It was a short walk in the pasture to where the dead calf was lying. During that walk, I questioned the owner about his feeding practices, how many cows he owned, how long he had raised cattle, how many calves had died, had they been sick long, etc. I learned that this was the third calf that had died, and the calves were about two weeks old -- a few were older, and a few were younger.

I honed my post mortem knife before I started the autopsy procedure to determine what had killed the calf. I followed the usual procedure for an autopsy--examining the abdominal organs, the organs in the chest, and checking the lymph nodes in the shoulder and groin areas. There were no lesions that told me what had killed the calf.

When I stuck my knife into the pail of water and disinfectant to wash it, I knew what had killed the calf. I saw oil that had come from the knife blade floating on top of the water.

"Your calf died of lead poisoning," I said to the farmer. "Where do you keep your used crankcase oil?"

"There's no used crankcase oil on this place," he replied.

Darkness was nearly upon us, so I told him I would return the next morning to seek out the source of the lead.

The farmer met me at the farm the next morning, and we started searching. First we searched the shed where machinery was stored, the most likely place for used crankcase oil. That's where the farmer would change the oil in his tractors.

Then I noticed an open door on the pump house. The little house was about eight feet square and tall enough for a man to walk into. It was designed to protect the electric water pump which served the house and the tanks that provided drinking water for the cattle.

There was no light bulb in the socket hanging from the ceiling of the building, but there was enough light coming through the open door for me to see a five gallon plastic pail in one of the corners at the back of the building. I carried the pail to the doorway where I saw that it was about two-thirds full of used crankcase oil. The pail of oil had probably been in the building for several years, left there by the previous tenant.

When the farmhouse was occupied, the cattle were kept in the pasture. With no one living in the house, the cattle were allowed to roam the area around the buildings to graze and keep the weeds and grass from growing and save the farmer the trouble of mowing.

Had the door to the pump house been kept closed, there would have been no access to the used oil, and there would have been no loss of calves.

❧❧❧❧

Loss of young dairy calves was another problem that a farmer and I had to solve. One of my good dairy clients, the owner of a herd of eighty Jersey cows, called me out to his farm to help him find out why his young calves were dying.

It was in the spring, and young calves that had been kept in pens were now turned out to graze the grass and small weeds that were growing around the barn and other outbuildings.

This helped the farmer by eliminating the need for him to mow.

I must admit that this wasn't one of the neater farmsteads where I treated animals, but there was no better dairyman than Frank Baldwin.

There were a few piles of old lumber lying around, the remains of repair jobs on the barn and other buildings. There also were a few piles of bricks and concrete blocks from the same repair jobs. Situated among one of the piles of brick were three or four old car batteries which was not a problem in itself. However, the caps where water was poured into the batteries were missing. When it rained, as it often does in the spring, water collected in the lead plates. Apparently the taste of lead is attractive to calves, because the calves were licking the water through the small capless openings in the top of the batteries.

Removal of the batteries solved the mystery of the dying dairy calves.

ノノノ∟

The two previous cases of lead poisoning occurred in young calves.

In older calves or adults, it is usually more difficult to establish a diagnosis. More detective work has to be done because they move over a larger area and have access to areas that young calves do not.

Walt Leigh called because his Hereford calves "just didn't look right," so a young veterinarian I had recently hired rode with me out to his farm to "size things up."

There were ten or twelve cows and the same number of calves in the Leigh herd. The calves were about five months old, having been born in February, so they were still nursing the cows. They were also grazing on the grass in the pasture and barn lot where Walt had confined them for us to see. In addition, he fed them a little grain each day.

Walt was a good cattleman, but these calves were moving slowly and had a rough hair coat and did not look like his calves usually looked.

As we walked among the cows and calves, it was evident that some of the calves had diarrhea, and others did not. In fact, one calf was straining to pass manure, and what he did pass was somewhat hard. The manure of all the calves was dark.

We roped a couple of the calves so we could check their temperature but learned nothing as both calves' temperatures were normal.

As we were strolling around the lot, one of us -- I can't remember which -- noticed a wet spot on one of the legs of the gasoline tank stand. The wet spot was just below where the nozzle was hanging. We made a presumptive diagnosis of lead poisoning from the calves licking the gasoline that had dripped down on the metal leg.

Our suggestion to Walt was to get a new nozzle for his gas tank or keep his cattle out of the barn lot. I believe he opted to get a new nozzle.

The health and appearance of his calves improved once the source of lead was removed.

CHAPTER 14

Ted Hurlburt

I was in the business area of my animal hospital when Ted Hurlburt walked into the waiting room several years ago. As he came close to me, I hoped he would keep his business as short as possible, because he looked and smelled as if he had come directly from his cattle lot. Without as much as a good morning or a howdy do, He asked, "How long does it take for a fly egg to develop into a maggot?"

"At what temperature?" I asked him.

Without any hesitation, he replied, "Eighty degrees."

"Let me get my entomology book," I said to him as I started for my office in the back of the building to retrieve the book. Fearing he might follow me, I told him, "I'll be right back."

As I returned to the business office, keeping as much distance between us as possible, I asked him, "Why do you need this information?"

"I'm being sued by the State of Illinois for the improper disposal of a dead animal," he answered. "My neighbor saw a dead cow in the pasture and reported me to the state."

I had a pretty good idea which cow he was referring to. A few weeks before, Ted had called me to remove a retained placenta from a cow.

When I arrived I found a cow, down and unable to rise, in the pasture with a dead calf lying behind her. As I looked at the cow I thought to myself, this is a waste of time because the cow is nearly dead.

I did, however, put on a shoulder length obstetrical sleeve, lubricated it well, and inserted my hand into the cow's vagina. Immediately, I could tell the visible tissue wasn't afterbirth. It was a ruptured urinary bladder, and the urine was draining into the body cavity. The cow was dying from uremic poisoning.

I told Ted the problem and suggested, since there was no hope for the cow, that he should get his gun and put her out of her misery.

Most farmers would call the rendering works to pick up the carcass, but I was sure Ted would elect to bury the carcass himself to save the $15 pickup charge.

I had a suspicion that one of the Hurlburts, probably a son, had tried to help this cow have her calf and did more harm than good.

"Well, Ted, my entomology book says that at eighty degrees Fahrenheit a fly egg will develop into a maggot in twelve to twenty-four hours."

"Ha! Ha! I've gottem."

"What do you mean, you've got them?"

"The man from the state stood on the road, looked at the cow fifteen rods away (165 feet) through a pair of binoculars and claimed he could see maggots," said Ted.

The presence of maggots was proof that the cow had been dead at least three days, according to the state employee.

"I need to borrow that book to take and show the judge when I appear before him tomorrow," Ted said.

"Sorry, I don't allow anyone to borrow my books, but I will make you a copy of the table," I told Ted.

"Good enough," said Ted.

As I was walking back to my office to make the copy for Ted, I was thinking that Illinois law required dead animals to be disposed of within twenty-four hours. I was also thinking that, if I knew Ted, the cow had been lying dead in the pasture for more than twenty-four hours...maybe many more.

I was also wondering if I was doing the right thing by abetting Ted in his attempt to "beat the law."

But then, I thought, any good judge will see right through Ted's attempt to prove the "state man" wrong, and surely the complainant will have enough proof to rebut Ted's information.

I returned to the front of the building where Ted was waiting and handed him the paper I had copied. As I did so, I said to him, "Good luck tomorrow."

"How much do I owe you?" Ted asked.

"Nothing, Ted," I replied. "I have a license to practice veterinary medicine, but not law."

Ted reached in his pocket and pulled out a ten dollar bill which he placed on the counter of my business area, turned and walked out the door.

A few days later, I read in the local paper that Ted had "beaten the rap." On the basis of evidence presented, Ted was declared innocent of the charge of improper disposal of a dead animal.

Several years later when I was at Ted's farm treating cattle, he reminded me of the time I had saved him from being fined by the state due to "evidence presented." I said to him, "Ted, you and I both know that cow had been there for more than twenty-four hours."

He laughed and said, "You're right."

♪♪♪

I recall another time when Ted came to my office with another question, and it was, "What can you do for a prostate problem?"

Two weeks before, I had treated his eighteen year-old male Terrier dog for an enlarged prostate gland with an injection of a female hormone. I suppose Ted thought I could do the same for him.

"Isn't your dog any better, Ted?" I asked him.

"Oh, he's fine. I just wanted to know what you can do for me."

"Ted, I can treat your cattle, I can treat your horse, and I can treat your dog, but I can't treat you. You need a medical doctor."

"I know that, Doc, but I thought you would be cheaper," Ted responded.

Ted was a wealthy man who owned many acres of farmland, but he was a mite thrifty.

➤➤➤➤

When I was called to the Hurlburt farm to treat cattle, I never knew what to expect... like the time I was called to deliver a calf. When I saw the cow, I knew she had been in labor for some time, possibly days. I knew the calf was a breech presentation, because he was coming "palms up" as a veterinarian friend of mine would say. I could see the bottoms of two feet protruding out of the vulva.

The cow was completely worn out and was breathing hard. Obviously, the calf was dead. I placed a loop of obstetrical strap over each leg, just above the foot. Placing the u-shaped part of my fetal extractor up next to the cow's upper rear legs, I attached the cable to the strap and began to tighten up the cable. As I continued to work the jack to reel in the cable, the calf started to move. Inch by inch, I was slowly bringing the rear legs out through the cow's vulva. Moving the handle of the jack slowly, I was gently bringing the dead fetus out of the suffering cow. At last, the hips eased out of the birth canal. And then the rest of the body emerged, and the dead, putrefying calf lay in the straw.

The cow was worn out, dehydrated and hot. Her eyes were sunken from the dehydration. Who knows how long she had been in labor and had gone unnoticed by the Hurlburts? She needed to be treated with antibiotics and a lot of IV fluids, and then it was questionable if she would survive.

I explained the situation to Ted, and he asked, "Can I butcher her?"

"You're kidding, right?" I asked him.

"No, I want to butcher her," he replied.

I whipped out my thermometer and inserted it into the cow's rectum. When I pulled it out, it read one hundred six degrees.

"Ted, there are several reasons why I can't give you permission to take this cow to a slaughter house. Number one -- she's within forty-eight hours of giving birth to a calf, Number two -- her temperature is five degrees above normal. Add those to the fact that with her high temperature, she won't bleed out properly."

"Can I butcher her myself?" Ted asked.

I responded with, "I wouldn't eat that meat, and I don't think you should either."

No matter how many reasons I gave him for not butchering the cow, he insisted that he was going to do it. I reminded him that he would have to cut her up and wrap the meat himself because he could not take her to a slaughter house.

While Ted and I were talking, his sons were knocking boards out of the side of the barn so they could drag the cow outside. Their aim was to pull her out to an engine hoist to raise her up in the air by her rear feet. This was so the blood would drain out of the jugular veins more easily when they were slit open.

When they finally got the cow out under the engine hoist, Ted asked me, "Will you shoot her for me?"

"Do you see that barn over there, Ted?" I asked. "I probably couldn't hit it with a bullet if I tried." The barn was probably fifty feet away.

I hadn't fired a gun since December of 1955. I had just returned home after serving four years in the navy, and a friend who had just been discharged from the army asked me to go squirrel hunting with him. We had a good time reminiscing that day, but we only fired the guns once or twice and didn't hit anything.

Ted persisted, so I agreed to shoot the cow.

He went to the house and returned with a brand new twenty-two rifle and handed it to me and indicated it was loaded.

I motioned to the three of them to stand back. The cow was lying under the engine hoist on a concrete pad, and I didn't want to miss so badly that the bullet ricocheted and hit one of them.

One well placed shot in the forehead between the eyes was all it took. It was no great feat to hit the proper spot, after all I was only about four feet away.

When the cow was suspended by the hind legs from the engine hoist, I attempted to slit her jugular veins so she would bleed out prior to Ted's skinning her, and then removing her entrails. The minute I stuck the knife into the vein, I could tell the cow would not bleed properly -- all that came out was dark clotted blood.

Again, I attempted to convince Ted he should not eat the meat from the cow.

However, he was adamant, and when I left he was starting to remove the skin with what appeared to be a dull knife.

The rest of this story came to me from the owner of a slaughter house where Ted attempted to take the cow to be cut up and packaged.

According to the owner of the slaughter house, when Ted arrived with the cow, he asked him if he had permission from a veterinarian to bring her to be processed.

When Ted answered in the affirmative, the butcher asked, "Which one?"

Ted replied, "That feller here in town, I can't remember his name."

Lloyd, the slaughter house owner, then asked, "Where's your letter?"

"What letter?" asked Ted.

"Dr. Day always writes a letter, on his letterhead stationery, saying it is okay for me to take care of the butchering. If you don't have a letter, I can't butcher your cow."

Ted was in a jam, but somehow people like Ted manage to survive.

An employee of the slaughter house said to Ted, "If you have a place for me to work, I will cut the cow up for you." It so happened that Ted had a vacant house, without electricity, that they could use and the butcher agreed to work by lantern light.

As I was told, when the butcher was about half finished with cutting the cow up into steaks, roasts, etc., he was bitten by a spider. I don't know if he finished the job, or if he left the job unfinished to go to the emergency room at the local hospital. I do know, however, that he spent three days in the hospital.

And I have never learned whether or not the meat was edible.

A few years later, I was talking to the man who had cut up the cow for Ted, and I asked if he remembered the incident. His reply was, "Yes, that cow was hit by lightning."

Under my breath, I said, "The lightning bolt that a .22 caliber slug carries."

♪♪♪

Ted had two adult sons who were partners with him in the farming operation. One day when we were running the bull calves through the cattle chute to make steers out of them, Maynard had been very disrespectful to Ted. It was starting to grate on me, because I would never have talked to my father that way.

Finally, I said to Ted, "I need a piece of two by four lumber."

"How long?" Ted asked.

"About four feet."

"What do you need it for?"

"I'm gonna hit that kid in the head with it to teach him to respect you more."

That was obviously a hollow threat, but Maynard must have heard what I said because he didn't smart off to Ted anymore that day.

Ted must have liked what I said about respect that afternoon, for he even told other people about the incident.

♪♪♪

As Ted aged, the boys took over more of the management of the farms.

Once, Maynard phoned me to ask if I could run a test on a calf to determine if it had died of organophosphate poisoning.

"No," I answered. "Why do you want to know?"

"I had a sick baby calf that wouldn't nurse his mother, so I stuck my finger in his mouth to see if he would suck it. I may have had some organophosphate insecticide on my finger. If he got poisoned on that, I want to write the company that manufactured it and tell them."

"You would have to take the calf to either the University of Illinois or Purdue University Veterinary School Diagnostic Laboratory to have that test performed."

"Do you know of any other vet around here that can run that test?"

"No private practitioner can run the test."

"I don't want to take the calf to a state lab."

"Why not?"

"I want to skin the calf and use the hide to put on another calf so that the dead calf's mother will let it nurse her."

"You don't have to do that. Just put a lariat around the cow's abdomen in front of her udder, and snug it up tightly. Not too tight, or the cow will fall over. Then you can hold the calf up to her udder to nurse without fear of being kicked. After a couple of times, the cow will accept the calf as her own."

"I'll have to think about it."

Two days later, I received a phone call from a diagnostician at the Purdue Vet School Lab who informed me that the calf had not died of organophosphate poisoning, but of E. coli scours (diarrhea).

E. coli is a normal inhabitant of the gut of man and animals. The bacteria aid in the digestion of food, and are usually beneficial bacteria. In this case the barn probably was not bedded with straw, and the cow's udder was dirty from lying down in the manure.

When the calf nursed, he took the bacteria from manure on the cow's dirty teats into his digestive system and became overloaded with the bacteria. His diarrhea caused him to lose fluids and become dehydrated. Then he didn't have the strength to nurse. Had the owner been more observant of the condition of the barn and the condition of the calf, perhaps the calf would not have contracted diarrhea or could have been saved in the early stages of the disease.

I called Maynard to inform him of the cause of the calf's death.

"What can I do to prevent another calf from getting sick?" he asked.

"Well, you can start by cleaning your barn. Then you need to bed it well with fresh straw and keep it clean from now on."

He thanked me and hung up the phone.

I hoped they had straw to bed the barn, but I couldn't be sure. One other time when I had suggested very strongly that they put straw in the barn, I was told they didn't have any.

CHAPTER 15

The Living Creche

It was the custom of the Methodist Church we attended to hold the children's Christmas program on the Sunday evening preceding Christmas Day.

One year, it was decided to have a living creche outside the church. The animals displayed in the creche were a burro, a small calf and a goat. All these, and the trailer to haul them, were borrowed from a fellow who kept a menagerie of animals on a small farm just outside town.

After the service, the children wanted to see the animals. As our family was standing in front of the creche, one of our neighbors tapped me on the shoulder and asked, "Are they healthy, Doc?"

I replied, not realizing how prophetic the statement would be, "They are now, but I don't know about later."

We went home and were soundly asleep when, at midnight, the telephone rang. Groggily, I arose and answered it to hear:

"Doc, this is Berkley. I've got a burro with its hoof cut off that I would like you to see."

"Is this the burro that was at the church?" I asked.

"Yes."

"Okay, I'll be out in about a half hour."

"No, I'll bring it to your office. I don't want to pay for a farm call."

Unbeknownst to him was the fact that he was going to pay for a call no matter where I saw the burro.

Then I said, "Bring it here to the house."

BIG MISTAKE!!

About a half hour later, I heard VROOM, VROOM, VROOM, as he backed his mufflerless car into our driveway. I'm sure half the neighborhood were awakened by the noise.

I'm not sure what I expected to see, but what I saw was not what I expected. Berkeley had the reputation of stretching the truth, so I didn't really believe him when he said the burro's hoof had been cut off.

He dropped the tailgate, which was hinged at the bottom, to make a ramp for the animals to walk up to get into the trailer. Blood completely covered the floor of the trailer.

It was then I deduced that when the tailgate was raised to haul the animals back home, the burro had his foot in the space between the floor and the tailgate. He either jerked his leg and pulled off the hoof, or the gate pinched it off when the men closed it.

Retrieving antibiotic ointment, a roll of cotton, gauze and tape from my truck, I bandaged the lower leg. I then gave the burro an injection of penicillin.

"I'll be out in the morning to change the bandage and give the burro a shot of tetanus antitoxin," I told Berkley.

The next morning, as promised, I went to the Berkley farm and treated the burro.

I knew that it would take six months for the hoof to grow back, and all that time the hoof would have to be protected from getting infected. I didn't feel that Berkley had enough ambition or stick-to-it-iveness to keep the hoof bandaged.

"How much is this burro worth?" I asked.

"I paid fifty dollars for him to breed my pony mares, but he won't do the job."

"Would you sell him to the church for fifty dollars?"

It was my idea that the church would purchase the donkey and then have him humanely disposed of. I figured this would cost a lot less than dealing with "Abe" Barkley. I had seen some of the shenanigans he had pulled in the past.

"I'd have to give that a lot of thought," Abe replied.

On my way to my office, I stopped at the church. When I asked for the pastor, I was told by the secretary that he was out. "I need to talk to him about the Berkley burro," I told her.

"He's going out to talk to Mr. Berkley today."

"Don't let him do that. If the pastor goes out to talk to him, Mr. Berkley will own this church building. It would be wiser to send the insurance man out to see him."

Apparently that's what happened because Abe Berkley showed up at my office the next morning wanting bandages and salve. He was going to bandage the foot himself, something he had refused to do up to now. In addition, he paid his bill of six months standing.

The insurance company paid him for the burro, paid the veterinary bill and allowed him to keep the animal. How much they paid for the burro, I don't know but it was probably more than Abe paid for him.

About six months later, I was at the Berkley place treating a horse when I asked, "Abe, whatever happened to your hoofless burro?"

He pointed to a small pasture north of the house and said, "There he is."

And there he was, standing on all four feet and grazing grass.

CHAPTER 16

Wild Things

Some railroad workers were repairing rails north of town after a train derailment when they came upon seven baby weasels in a nest. The mother was nowhere to be found, so the men brought the babies to my office.

A weasel is a small carnivore of the Mustelidae family, which also includes ferrets, stoats, mink and ermine.

The body of the weasel is very long and slender which enables them to slip easily through a hole into a chicken house to make their nighttime raids.

I called the District State Police Headquarters and they contacted the game warden. He said he could not come for the weasel babies until the following day to take them to the University Of Illinois College Of Veterinary Medicine Wildlife Rehabilitation Center.

After agreeing to care for the kits until he arrived, I realized it would be necessary for someone to feed them several times during the night. I could see that I wouldn't get much sleep that night.

Much to my relief Sarah, one of my employees, agreed to come to the office during the night for some of the feedings.

I couldn't get those babies out of the waiting room fast enough because there was a very strong musty odor about them and their nesting material.

Providing feed for the baby weasels would not be a problem because we kept on hand a supply of milk replacement for kittens. We also had a supply of kitten feeding bottles.

We fed the weasel kits at six p.m. when we closed the office for the night.

Sarah fed the babies at nine p.m., I did it at midnight and so on.

When the game warden came the next morning to get the little weasels, he told me I should have had the railroad worker take the babies back to where he had found them.

My reply to that advice was, "I had four clients sitting in my waiting room when the weasels were brought in. If I had told the man that, I probably would have lost four clients."

♪♪♪

By providing veterinary services for an exotic animal farm and petting zoo, I have had some experiences that other veterinarians haven't.

For instance, I had the opportunity to perform pregnancy exams on four Yaks.

This long haired shaggy animal from Asia is related to the American buffalo and is used as a beast of burden on that continent. The females are somewhat smaller than our buffalo females.

Performing a pregnancy exam on a Yak is done the same as on a cow or mare. The hand, encased in a well lubricated plastic shoulder length sleeve, is inserted into the rectum. The fingers are used to palpate (feel) the uterus and ovaries through the wall of the rectum. If the female is pregnant, the uterus will be enlarged. If she is not, the uterus will be small and eggs may be palpated (felt) on the ovaries. If the uterus is gravid (pregnant) the approximate age of the fetus may be determined.

None of the four were pregnant, and none of the four were ovulating.

They did have really strong odor about them...even worse than the weasels.

I don't know if that was their natural odor, or if they had acquired it from sleeping with male goats.

I was also exposed to fainting goats at the petting zoo.

A fainting goat is a domestic goat whose muscles freeze for about ten seconds when the goat feels panic. Though painless, this generally results in the animal collapsing on its side. This characteristic is caused by an hereditary genetic disorder called myotonia congenita.

If a loud noise occurs, a younger goat will stiffen and fall over. An older goat has learned to spread its legs or lean against some object when they are startled.

I have seen a young goat stiffen and fall on its side just because he jumped over a board about four inches high.

Fainting goats are slightly smaller than most goats.

I saw my first Vietnamese potbellied pig at the Horse Farm and Petting Zoo when I neutered him.

At that time the pig which was supposed to stay small, in comparison to the domestic swine of our country, was just coming into popularity in this country. They were touted to be the condo pet of the future. Owners are able to train their pigs to use a litter box. Potbellied pigs are very intelligent, as are our domestic swine, and become bored when left alone in a condo all day. Thus, they sometimes become destructive.

Another disadvantage of these pigs was the difficulty in getting them to a veterinarian for their vaccinations, hoof trimming, etc., because of their size.

Potbellied pigs have declined in popularity since twenty-five years ago.

When I was in veterinary college, I never dreamed that one day I would be treating buffalo.

That's exactly what happened when one of my clients, who raised beef cattle, decided to go into the American Buffalo breeding business.

He ran a breeding to finish operation. The fifty cows he owned gave birth to calves which he put into the feedlot and fattened for slaughter.

Buffalo meat is desired by people who want high protein with little fat. Much of the meat from calves slaughtered locally was sold to members of the Chicago Bears football team.

I learned early that one cannot herd a buffalo in any certain direction. A person just starts a buffalo in the direction they want them to go and hopes they continue to go there.

An angry buffalo will charge a large tractor.

After waiting for an injection of tranquilizer to take effect on my first call to deliver a buffalo calf, I dispensed a bottle of tranquilizer to the client for his use prior to calling me.

Once, the farmer engaged me to test fifty buffalo cows for brucellosis and tuberculosis. The animals were being shipped to a Nebraska pasture to graze and Nebraska law required that they be negative for the two diseases.

I anticipated the testing to require most of the day to complete. It was necessary for the tuberculin to be injected into the fold of the skin under the tail, while the blood had to be drawn from the jugular vein in the big neck of the animal. If I were drawing blood from a cow, I would use the caudal vein under the tail. However, if one held a cow's tail up over her back, she would not or could not kick. This wasn't true of a buffalo, so tail bleeding was out of the question.

Since the sides of the stanchion had to be opened wide to allow the broad head of a buffalo to pass through before they were closed on the neck, it was necessary to have a hinged cage over the front of the head gate. Once the animal was caught, the cage could be swung back to allow access to the head of the buffalo.

The next step in the testing process was to check the inside of the right ear for an identification tattoo and a vaccination tattoo. The identification number would be written down on the test papers to identify that particular animal while the vaccination tattoo would indicate if and when the animal had been vaccinated against brucellosis. If no ID number was evident in the ear, a metal identification tag would be placed in the top of the right ear.

In order for blood to be drawn from the right jugular vein, the head must be pulled around to the left and held there long enough for the procedure to be carried out.

This job fell to one of the farmer's sons. He would place his body next to the big shaggy head and lean against it to force it to the right and hold it while I drew the blood sample. This was quite a task and, after we had finished, I told him he must be the strongest man in the county. The other son, who had been moving the buffalo into the chute, jokingly took umbrage at that statement. I then told him that he might be the handsomest.

Seventy-two hours later we ran the fifty animals through the chute again so I could check the tuberculin injection sites for swelling which would indicate that the cow was infected with tuberculosis.

There were no TB reactors, and the blood samples were all negative for brucellosis, so the buffalo cows could be slipped to Nebraska.

Our son, Jim, and I were watching a sports event on TV one Sunday afternoon when a call came that my lone Chinchilla client had a female that could not have her little ones.

As we drove to the office I was thinking about John and his Chinchilla business. John raised the animals to be sold for fur.

He owned a small construction business and had built his own housing for the Chinchillas. The building was very modern with underground pipes running out in several directions. The pipes were buried three feet deep except at the entry where the air came in. Since the temperature at about that distance below the ground stays near seventy degrees Fahrenheit year round, John was able to maintain a constant and optimal temperature year round for his Chinchillas.

The Chinchilla is native to the Andes region of South America and their pelts have been used as furs for years. They are an expensive fur. I saw a man's jacked listed for $25,000.

John placed the animal on the table for me to examine. Fluids were dripping from the vulva of the little animal. There wasn't much examining I could do to an animal that was about a foot long and weighed no more than a pound and a half. Concerned for the animal's health, John asked if I could help her.

I had never done a Caesarean section on anything that small, but I suggested to John that the surgery was worth a try.

We placed the animal in a holding cage while we got ready for surgery. One of our neighbors was a nurse anesthetist at the local hospital, and he had recently supplied me with two small bottles of ketamine hydrochoride, a new non barbiturate anesthetic. It appealed to me because I could inject it intramuscularly which was a plus in an animal that small.

I injected the minute amount of the drug needed into the muscle of the tiny animal.

Shortly, the animal was down on its side with its eyes wide open. In fact, the eyes never closed during or after the surgery. I learned that is one of the characteristics of the drug.

After the usual clipping and disinfecting of the skin, I placed a sterile drape over the area to be incised. I opened the abdominal wall and brought the uterus outside the body.

The first tiny Chinchilla baby I brought out of the uterus, I handed to my son who was standing by with a towel. As he tried to dry the wriggling little animal, it kept popping out of the towel. The tail was as long as the body and the whiskers as long as the tail. The anesthetic had not affected the baby animal at all.

After the second baby was delivered, I sutured the uterus, body wall, and the skin to complete the job and placed the female and the young ones in the cloth lined box in which she had been brought to my office.

A phone call to John brought him immediately to my hospital from his home a few blocks away.

The pleased smile on his face, when he saw the mother and two babies, told me that we had done a good job.

֍֍֍֍

It was another Sunday afternoon when I was called to see a different kind of patient…a small monkey.

Up to this time, I had not had a monkey as a patient and my knowledge of monkey medicine was practically zero. The monkey would have probably been better served by a medical doctor.

When the owner walked into my office with his monkey wrapped in a blanket, I thought the little animal was dead. His head flopped to the side and he couldn't lift it. His eyes were also closed.

Before I allowed the owner to place the monkey on the table, I inserted my thermometer into his rectum. When I withdrew it, I could see that the reading was five degrees below normal. The little guy was nearly dead.

I asked the owner to please have a seat in the waiting room and hold the monkey tight while we prepared to treat him. While I warmed a bottle of intravenous saline-dextrose solution, I asked Jim, my son, to get the heating pad from the storeroom.

The bottle of fluids was still warming in hot running water when I plugged in the heating pad and placed it on the table. With the monkey still wrapped in his blanket, we placed him on the heating pad.

As soon as I had the fluid slightly warmer than body temperature, I inserted a small gauge needle into the tiny vein of the monkey's right arm and taped it in place. With the bail of the bottle hanging on the arm of an I.V. stand, I adjusted the intravenous tube to a very slow drip.

We continued the slow intravenous drip for three hours, and the monkey slowly came out of his stupor.

I occasionally checked his temperature and as it rose, he awakened more.

Finally, after four hours, his temperature was normal and he was awake and moving.

At that time, we sent him home wrapped in his warm blanket.

I will never know what caused the little monkey to go into such deep shock.

॥॥॥

My second monkey patient was a different story.

His owner, a high school student, stopped into my office and told me his monkey had diarrhea.

I suggested he bring me a sample of the monkey's feces.

The next day, the young man dropped the fecal sample at my office on his way to school.

I examined the feces under my microscope and saw Strongyloides eggs. This is not a common intestinal parasite in our area.

The only medicine I had to kill those worms had an active ingredient of iodine, which caused the animal to defecate purple...and it produced stains. I dispensed the medicine, with instructions, to the young man on his way home from school.

The next day, the young man stopped in again and asked, "Why didn't you tell me that he would leave purple stains all over the kitchen where he defecated?"

I asked, "Why didn't you tell me you don't keep him in a cage?"

॥॥॥

While this isn't exactly a story of a wild pig; it could have been.

Bob Morgan brought two small pigs to my office to have inguinal hernia surgery performed on them. Since they were small, he confined them in a poultry crate in the bed of his pickup truck.

As it was a warm spring day, we were doing the surgery outside the rear door of my animal hospital.

As Bob opened the top of the wooden crate to replace the first pig, the other pig managed to escape the crate, climbed over the side of the pickup bed and headed for the highway. Since Bob had his hands full of pig, and my hands were full of surgical instruments, there wasn't much we could do.

When we saw the pig wasn't going to stop, we started to chase him. Soon, he was headed for the river with Bob and me in hot pursuit. After about an eighth of a mile Bob said, "Forget him, Doc." We turned and headed back to my office.

Bob left for home with his one pig, and I left on a farm call.

To my amazement, when I returned from my farm call, the pig was lying outside the back door of my office.

The prodigal pig had returned.

Apparently he changed his mind about becoming a feral pig and roaming the countryside.

I took the pig into my surgery room and tied him to the surgery table. After using a line block of local anesthetic, I repaired the inguinal hernia and castrated the pig.

Bob was much surprised when I called and told him he could pick up his wandering pig.

꙳꙳꙳꙳

I had just arrived at my animal hospital on a Saturday morning when Rob Tamblen came flying up in his pickup truck. I could tell it was him by the gas tank in the bed of his truck. He used the gas tank to supply his construction equipment.

He had a little difficulty getting in the door because he was carrying a little fawn in his arms.

"Can you help this poor little girl?" he asked.

I could see blood on Rob's shirt sleeve and the right foreleg of the fawn.

"Put her on the exam table," I said to Rob.

As the fawn lay on the table, I could see the bloody stump of her right leg, cut off just below the knee.

"What happened?" I asked.

With tears in his eyes, Rob told me he was mowing hay and didn't see the fawn nestled down in the clover until he had mowed her leg off.

"Can you save her?" asked Rob.

"Oh, yes, I can save her, but I doubt she can ever be turned out to fend for herself again," I told him.

"We'll worry about that after we get her well," he said.

I amputated the leg at the knee joint, and Rob took her home with him. I was sure he would fix the fawn a nice pen in his horse barn.

A week later when Rob brought the fawn for suture removal, he told me that he called the State Conservation Department and received permission to keep the fawn in a pen on his farm.

When I vaccinated Rob's two horses a year later, I saw the fawn in her pen with her own little shelter. She was so fat she could barely walk.

Rob sold his horses a short time later, so I never saw the fawn again.

CHAPTER 17

Carl Dingleberry

"This is Carl Dingleberry," the voice on the other end of the line said as I answered the phone. "The county vet was out and tested the kids' calves for the fair, and he said I should call you to come out and take a look at one of the steers."

"What's wrong with the steer?" I asked.

"He's got a swelling under his belly," Carl replied.

Carl was waiting for me when I drove into his barnyard about an hour later. "The steer's tied up in the barn." Carl said.

"Will you please bring him outside where I can see better?" I asked.

Carl led the well-broken steer out of the barn and tied him to the wooden fence.

I saw that the swelling extended from in front of the steer's scrotum all the way to between the front legs and was about three inches thick.

"Have you done anything to this steer recently?" I asked.

"I felt his scrotum a few days ago, and I thought there was part of a testicle in there, so I clamped him again."

Clamping refers to a method of closed castration with an instrument called an emasculatome. According to the Merriam-Webster dictionary an emasculatome, *is a pair of double hinged pincers for castrating domestic animals bloodlessly by crushing the spermatic cord through the unbroken skin.* (Unbroken skin of his scrotum, I would add).

An emasculatome may only be used on animals with a pendulous scrotum, i.e., cattle, goats or sheep -- not dogs, cats, pigs, or horses.

If a poor job of clamping is done and some testicular tissue remains, the animal will show some of the characteristics of an un-castrated male or bull and is called a "stag." This steer did not show the bullish head, or the pendulous penile sheath, so there was no need to have clamped him again.

I felt the swelling under the abdomen. It was soft and pitted (meaning a small depression was left) when I pushed on it with one of my fingers.

I retrieved a sixteen gauge bleeding needle from my truck and inserted it through the skin. Urine dripped out of the needle.

"Well, Carl, I believe you clamped this steer's penis, and a cut in the penis developed at the site where you placed the clamps. Urine is running out through the cut and is collecting between the skin and the muscle."

"Can you do anything for the steer?" asked Carl.

"I can make a female out of him. I'm going to make an incision on the midline between the rear legs about half way between the anus and the scrotum. Then I'm going to bring the penis to the out-side and cut it into two parts. The lower part we'll leave in place, and the upper part we'll suture to the skin, and the steer will forever after urinate between the rear legs." After completing the surgery, known as a perineal urethrostomy, I turned my attention to the fluid trapped between the skin and muscle of the abdomen.

With a scalpel, I made several pairs of small slits in the skin of the un-derbody. Using umbilical tape and a long curved suture needle, I placed loops through each of the paired slits and tied knots in them. Umbilical tape is gauze about one-half inch wide, and these loops would act as wicks and allow the urine to drain by dripping from between the muscle and the skin. This is commonly known as "drip drying."

I feared that the collection of urine pooled between the skin and muscle for so long a time might cause some of the skin to die and slough off. However, when I removed the loops of umbilical tape a week later, the skin was totally healthy.

The steer had to miss a trip to the fair and a possible blue ribbon, however.

I hoped Carl had learned a lesson and would be more careful when he clamped calves in the future. But no, a couple of years later, he brought me three small calves on which he had managed to clamp the penis…same surgery, smaller patients.

◆ ◆ ◆

Carl also had a saddle horse that I was called to see one day. He was good at telling me what was wrong with his animals when he phoned. This time his provisional diagnosis was a "belly ache" because the horse was not eating.

When I arrived at the Dingleberry farm, Carl showed me to where the horse was tied in the barn and left with the excuse he had something else to take care of.

While I was checking the horse's temperature with a rectal thermometer, I noticed that the tail was sticking out parallel to the floor of the barn. This wasn't normal unless the horse was trying to have a bowel movement and this wasn't the case. I doubled up my fist and hit the horse gently on the rump, and the muscle felt like a brick wall. I then went to the horse's head to examine its mouth, which it could not open.

I had my diagnosis--- tetanus, or lockjaw.

Horses are very susceptible to lockjaw. I have saved some Shetland pony foals who were infected by the bacteria entering the body through their navel cord, but my attempts to cure an adult horse of the condition had been futile.

I hunted for Carl and when I found him, I said, "Well, your horse doesn't have a belly ache like you thought."

Ever the optimist, Carl asked, "Oh, just a little colic, huh?"

"No, he has lockjaw. I will load him up with penicillin and leave some for you to give him, but I'm afraid it's a hopeless cause." I also gave him a quadruple dose of tetanus antitoxin intravenously.

꜀꜀꜀꜀

It was a Saturday afternoon and a time to relax when I received another call from Carl. "I've got fat steers over here that are scratching themselves to death. They just stand and rub their rear ends on the wooden fence or the side of the barn until they're raw."

I was pretty sure I knew the problem, but I told him I would come over to his farm and take a look at the steers.

When I arrived at the Dingleberry farm, I was surprised to see some really thin Hampshire sows running around the barn lot. To my knowledge, Carl had not had hogs for years.

"How long have you had these hogs, Carl?" I asked.

"Just got 'em last week," he replied. "Joseph Bailey came by with a bunch of thin sows, and I figured I could make some money letting them 'run behind' the feed lot cattle."

"Running behind" the feedlot cattle means letting the hogs glean the undigested kernels of corn from the cattle manure.

I thought to myself, you're not going to make any money from these hogs; they're the reason you're going to lose a bunch of money.

I really didn't want to burst Carl's bubble about making money on these hogs, but I had to do it. "Carl, your cattle have pseudorabies, or 'mad itch', and they're going to die. Pseudorabies (also known as Aujeszky's disease) is a viral disease and is spread from infected swine to cattle. Joseph didn't do you any favors when he sold you these thin sows, and if he knew these hogs had pseudorabies, he could be in trouble with the Illinois Department of Agriculture."

I returned home and called the state veterinarian at his home and got him out of the shower. He took the information and said he would send an inspector up to Carl's place on Monday to put a quarantine in place on both farms.

As it turned out, Carl lost four fat steers. His loss was many times what he would have made on the sows had he fattened them. He was required, by the state, to sell the sows for slaughter immediately.

Joseph Bailey didn't have an Illinois Livestock Dealers' License, but he was fined only fifty dollars by the state. It didn't seem to me that the punishment fit the crime. He cost Carl Dingleberry hundreds of dollars by selling him hogs that rightfully should have been sent to slaughter.

CHAPTER **18**

Cat Tales

Some of the most interesting experiences in my veterinary practice involved cats and their owners.

One time a lady phoned me and said she had just run her kitten through a cycle in her clothes dryer and asked if I would be able to see the kitten. Surprised that the kitten was still alive, I suggested she come immediately.

The kitten she placed on the examination table had probably weighed about four pounds prior to its ride in the tumbling clothes dryer, but now weighed considerably less due to severe dehydration -- in effect, she had dried the kitten out like her clothes.

When I took a pinch of the kitten's skin between my thumb and forefinger, lifted and released, the skin had no elasticity and remained standing.

I immediately began subcutaneous administration of sterile saline solution to replace the fluids the kitten had lost due to being dried like wet clothes. Intravenous injection of the fluids would have accomplished the results I desired more rapidly, but I doubted I could insert a needle in a vein because of the severe loss of fluids and the small size of the kitten.

Once I had the treatment started, I could relax a little, so I began the conversation to find out why the kitten had been in the clothes dryer. The owner related to me that, as she was heading to the bathroom to take a shower, she noticed the door of the dryer was open and, as she walked by, slammed the door shut. After showering, as she walked back past the dryer, she heard a thumping noise that sounded like a sneaker going around as the clothes tumbled. When she opened the door, instead of a shoe, she saw the kitten and immediately phoned me.

Fortunately, the treatment was successful, and the kitten recovered and grew into a nice healthy cat. However, I'm not sure the owner ever recovered from the embarrassment of closing the door of the clothes dryer with her kitten inside.

♪♪♪♪

One of my other clients closed the oven door of her kitchen range and turned on the heat with her Siamese cat inside. Fortunately, she didn't leave the room and immediately opened the door when cat began making distressed noises. The only harm to the cat was shorter whiskers and singed eyelashes.

♪♪♪♪

When I first opened my practice, we lived about three miles north of town and across the major highway from our home sat a large barn. I usually had my walk-in hours for pets from four to six in the evening as I was busy making farm visits during the day. One evening in the late fall as a client was carrying his cat to his car, a large truck passed on the highway and frightened the cat, causing it to jump from the man's arms and scamper across the road to the barn. A cursory attempt at finding the cat on the other side of the road without any lights was unsuccessful, so the owner went home thinking he had lost his pet.

Two nights later, we heard cat noises outside the door of our house and thought it was our cat, Soxie, wanting to be let in. When I went to the door, I found the client's cat standing by the door of my examining room.

The owner was ecstatic when I phoned him and told him he could come for his cat, because the escapee had returned.

❧ ❧ ❧

One day around five a.m., I received a call from a farmer requesting my services.

One of his Angus cows had "thrown out her uterus after calving," and he wanted me to "put it back in her."

I drove to the farm which was about nine miles from our home where I completed the task of replacing the uterus and, about an hour later, drove back into town and stopped at a filling station to gas up my car. As I walked past the front of the car to go into the station to tell the attendant how much gas I wanted (that's right, we actually had people who would pump our gas, wash our windows, and check our oil back then), I noticed some black and white hairs protruding through the grill. I thought a skunk had crawled onto my fender while I was at the farm. I gingerly opened the hood, thinking I could be sprayed by the skunk at any minute.

Much to my surprise and glee, I saw our black and white cat, Soxie, peering out at me from the top of the right fender. He had ridden from our home to the farm and had stayed perched in his spot on the fender while I treated the cow. Thankfully, he had not gone exploring while I was at the farm.

I retrieved the frightened cat from his spot on the fender and placed him on the seat beside me and drove home for breakfast. Apparently Soxie did not enjoy his ride, because he never tried that trick again.

❧ ❧ ❧

Another one of my cat tales involved our youngest son, Jim (or Jimmy as he was called when he was a small boy).

Jimmy's best friend, Frank, lived across the street from our house. His family decided they needed a larger home, so they built a new home on the edge of town.

A new home also meant a new puppy for Frank that he was anxious for Jimmy to see. We gave Jimmy our permission to go home with Frank after school. It was a cold, winter day, and there was a bit of snow on the ground. They walked past the local hospital on their way to Frank's house. When they saw a dead cat lying in the hospital parking lot, Jimmy picked it up and was carrying it.

A lady, who lived near Frank, saw the boys walking and stopped to give them a ride. When she saw the dead cat that Jimmy was carrying, she asked what they were going to do with it. Jimmy replied, "My Dad's a veterinarian, and he can fix him up."

The lady exclaimed, "But he's dead."

Jimmy answered, "Yes, and he's froze too."

Although Jimmy's blind faith in my abilities as a veterinarian was greatly exaggerated, he at least used good sense in borrowing Frank's gloves to carry the cat.

♪♪♪

The eight year old son of our friends was at the baby sitter's house when he told her, "We took our cat to Dr. Day to have her pianos removed."

The baby sitter asked, "Phillip, don't you mean her organs?"

"That's right", Phillip replied, "I knew it was some kind of musical instrument."

♪♪♪

Our daughter's family had a calico cat called Patches that I had gotten for them from a client of mine. Patches was a nice cat, but she had wandering fever. When let out of the house for some outside exercise, she had a habit of disappearing. Once, an elderly neighbor lady let the cat into her house, and Patches stayed for several days.

To prevent Patches from roaming through the neighborhood when they let her outside, they began tying the cat to a long rope that was attached to a stake. One day when the children came home from school, my daughter asked her oldest child, Mindy, to bring the cat into the house. As Mindy carried the cat into the family room, she said, "Look, Mom! Patches has a flower in her mouth."

Surprise! Surprise! What appeared to be the stem of a flower protruding from the cat's mouth was actually the tail of a mouse -- discovered when Patches yawned and the mouse jumped out and ran under the television set. And that's where the mouse stayed until the father came home from work and retrieved the mouse. He didn't kill it, just carried it outside and let it go free.

With four kids, two cats and a dog loose in that house, I can understand why the mouse stayed under the TV set.

ﬞﬞﬞﬞ

One of my feline patients was a neutered black male with the strange name of Yuck.

Yuck's owner, B. J., was the owner of a local tavern and was an interesting individual.

B. J. was an Army Air Corps fighter pilot during World War II, and I sometimes thought he was up in the wild blue yonder yet. He still wore his leather flying jacket in the winter, complete with Air Corps emblems sewn to it.

Yuck normally was a healthy cat, so I usually only saw him for his annual vaccinations

One day, though, B. J. and Yuck were the first ones to show up at my walk-in hours which started at four p. m.

As B. J. placed Yuck on the examination table, I asked, "What's the matter with Yuck, B. J?"

"He won't eat, Doc," B. J. replied.

When I started to do the physical exam, I noticed that Yuck's eyes were dull and his hair coat was not shiny and smooth as it usually is in a healthy cat. He had lost three pounds since his previous visit.

Moving to the rear to take Yuck's temperature, I noticed about four inches of fine white thread protruding from Yuck's anus.

Jokingly, I asked, "B. J., do you do much needle work?" The reply was, "No, but Jenny does." Jenny was B. J.'s live in companion. "Why do you ask?"

"Because Yuck swallowed a needle."

"How can you tell that?" asked B. J.

"There is a thread about four inches long hanging from Yuck's anus."

It is amazing to me that a needle, swallowed by the cat, passed down the esophagus and through the stomach and about twenty-five feet of small and large intestine before lodging in the rectum.

I tugged gently on the thread to no avail. Something was preventing the needle from passing the rest of the way. Fearing that I would do irreparable damage to the colon or rectum if I exerted enough force to dislodge the needle, I told B. J. that I needed to surgically remove it.

B. J. readily agreed to the surgery, so we placed Yuck in a holding cage until I could do the surgery.

Not wanting to wait until the next day for surgery, as soon as my office hours ended, we took Yuck to the surgery room. Since he wasn't eating, we would not need to hold him off feed before anesthetizing him.

After the usual preparation and anesthetization, I opened Yuck's abdomen and brought the rectum outside through the midline incision. As soon as I saw the rectum, I was glad that I had decided to do surgery. The needle had penetrated the wall and there was a small gangrenous area around the needle. I also saw that the needle was imbedded in a mass of dried feces which was too large to enter the pelvic canal.

Removal of the fecal mass and needle was uneventful once I had made a large enough incision in the wall of the rectum. After trimming the small area of gangrene from the intestinal wall, I sutured the wound. Following this, I closed the incision in the abdominal wall.

The next morning, Yuck was wide awake and hungry. I placed a small amount of canned food in a bowl, and, as I placed it in the cage, Yuck almost bit my hand getting to the food. His appetite returned to normal once the obstructing fecal mass and needle were removed.

B. J. came to get Yuck in the afternoon, and when I told him the bill was thirty five dollars, he replied in his cocky way, "I would have bet it would be a half a hundred."

This was in the late 1960's and, neither veterinary fees nor medical fees were as astronomical as they are now. As a matter of fact, I believe gasoline prices were below fifty cents a gallon.

When I removed the skin sutures a week later, B. J. reported Yuck as being himself again.

❧❧❧❧

I was surprised when a lady who had once been our neighbor showed up one afternoon during office hours with an adult cat. I didn't even know she owned a cat.

I greeted her, and since I knew they had recently moved to a new house on a farm they owned asked her, "How are things down on the farm?" She laughed and said, "Just fine."

My receptionist said Wanda wants to leave her cat to be neutered and declawed. The next day was one of my surgery days, and I knew the cases were light, so I said, "okay."

As my receptionist was entering the cat's information into the computer, I asked Wanda, "Where did you get the cat?"

"It's a stray that just came to our house, and I'm giving it to our daughter, Linda."

On the farm where she and her husband lived was a small tenant house that they rented out. I knew that a few weeks before the renters had moved to another state. I also knew that those tenants owned several cats.

I asked, "Do you think this could be one of the cats belonging to the people who just moved out of your rental house?"

"Oh, I don't think so," she replied.

"I just wanted to make sure."

I later found out that the lady who had previously lived in the rental house did return to inquire if one her cats had "come home."

◢◢◢

When I voted in the last election, the young lady who handed me my ballot asked, "Are you Dr. Day?"

I replied, "Yes."

She said, "You probably won't remember this, but when I was a little girl, my aunt and I brought my little kitten to you. The kitten had been hit by a car and was badly injured."

"You took the kitten to a room at the back of your hospital, and when you returned, you asked my aunt to phone you the following day."

"When my aunt phoned the following day, she was told we could come and get the kitten."

"It was only about six months ago that my aunt told me the real story. You knew you couldn't save the kitten, but you knew where you could get one the same sex, size, color and approximate age. You didn't want me to be hurt by the loss of my kitten, so you gave me a replacement that I thought was really my kitten."

I had forgotten this particular incident, but as I now recall it, my long time employee, Wilma Craft, had a litter of kittens at the time. She supplied the replacement kitten.

◢◢◢

One Sunday afternoon, I received a frantic phone call from the wife of one of our most prominent citizens. After identifying herself, she said, "Doctor, you just have to see our cat. She's in great pain."

I agreed to meet her at my office in fifteen minutes time.

When the two cat owners walked into my office with a squalling cat, I remembered a question I should have asked when I was on the phone, "Is your cat rolling and rubbing around on the floor?"

As the lady placed the cat on the exam table, I asked the question.

"Yes," they both replied.

"Your cat is in heat," I told them.

Both were somewhat embarrassed and asked if they could leave the cat to be spayed, and I agreed.

❧❧❧

As I was vaccinating a dog for one of my clients, she said, "I have a cat that seems to be in misery all the time."

"Has she been spayed?" I asked, thinking it might be a long standing heat. Cats are spontaneous ovulators, meaning that they only go out of heat if they are spayed or bred.

Otherwise, they may go through periods of quiescence, but are still in heat and show the signs.

"She was spayed by an old veterinarian in southern Indiana where my folks lived about five years ago, and she has been nasty ever since."

"He probably left a piece of ovary when he did the surgery."

"Can you do anything about it?"

"I'll give it a try if you want to bring her over next Monday. We'll hold her off feed the night before and do surgery the next morning."

"Do you mind if I watch?"

"I guess it's okay if you promise not to faint when you see blood. Be here at nine a.m."

She brought the cat in the afternoon as I requested, and was at my office promptly at nine o'clock the next morning.

After anesthetizing the animal, we clipped her abdomen, cleaned and disinfected the surgical area, laid her on her back on the surgical table, and placed a surgical drape over her.

Grasping a scalpel in my gloved right hand, I made an incision about two inches long through the skin. A small amount of blood appeared and I looked at Marilyn, the owner of the cat. She was fine... her skin color was normal.

I then made an incision through the muscle and peritoneal layers of the body. Before starting surgery, I had tilted the table slightly with the cat's head lower than its tail. This would help keep the intestines out of my way when I searched for the ovarian tag.

Inserting the end of my spay hook into the body cavity, I searched where the ovary should have been. I snagged a piece of tissue and brought it outside the body. Eureka!!! With one try, I had managed to get hold of the ovarian tag. After placing a clamp on the tissue below the piece of ovary, I tied off the tissue with a suture below the clamp before removing the ovarian tag.

After suturing the three layers of tissue of the cat's body, we placed the animal in a cage to recover from the anesthetic.

We discharged the cat to Marilyn the following morning with instructions for her to return the following Tuesday afternoon during office hours for suture removal.

When owner and cat returned the following week for suture removal, the owner was beaming. She said, "Doc, this cat has always hated my Dad. When he came over to our house this week, she ran in and jumped up in his lap. Now, she's as sweet as she was as a kitten. Thank you, very much."

♪♪♪

When I was a child of about four years of age, I was given a female kitten.

At that time, there was an early morning show on radio station WLS called Smile Awhile. One of the stars of that show was a female singer who called herself Patsy Montana, and she was a favorite of mine.

Naturally, I named my kitten Patsy.

I doubt if my parents gave any consideration to having her spayed. Besides, it was the Great Depression, and we wouldn't have had the money to pay for neutering a cat.

As soon as Patsy reached puberty, some roaming tomcat found her and she became pregnant.

Patsy gave birth to a litter of kittens that were all killed by another roaming (or perhaps even their father) tomcat before their eyes were opened.

I discovered this one morning when I walked out our back door and found them where she had placed them on a step of our back porch.

Later, when I learned that a female cat comes in heat as soon as her kittens are weaned, I understood the tomcat's reason for killing the kittens.

Sexual gratification was more important to that male cat than propagating the species.

CHAPTER 19

Strange Appetites

I had not been in practice very long when I was presented with an eight year- old Boxer dog with a history of vomiting for several days. After a careful examination, I decided the dog had a foreign body in her stomach.

The next thing to do was take an x-ray of the dog's stomach. However, since I was just starting my practice, I had neither the money nor the space for an x-ray machine.

Therefore, I decided to refer the animal to a practice that did possess an x-ray machine, and I chose a group practice of three veterinarians about thirty-five miles away.

I instructed my client to tell the examining veterinarian my diagnosis and ask for an x-ray -- even a barium study if necessary. My thought was that if an object could not be seen on a normal x-ray, the use of barium in the stomach would outline the foreign object.

I didn't hear from my clients, so I concluded the problem had been resolved. While attending a meeting of a regional veterinary association about three weeks later, I met one of the veterinarians in the group where I had referred the dog. He said to me, "Well, we found the foreign body in the Boxer's stomach -- it was a baby nipple."

"Did you find it on x-ray?" I asked. "No, we found it during the post mortem exam after the dog died," he replied.

I tried hard not to show my disappointment because I knew the dog shouldn't have been allowed to die. One or two diagnostic x-rays and surgery to remove the nipple, and my clients would have still had their dog.

❧❧❧❧

Dogs and cats are not the only animals that swallow strange objects. Cattle, especially dairy cattle, are notorious for having "hardware" in the second part of their four part stomach -- the reticulum.

I have removed nails, nuts, bolts, pieces of chicken wire fence, razor blades, and fence staples (and those are only the ones I can remember) out of dairy cows' stomachs.

A cow or bull is not very selective in what they pick up from the barnyard or pasture.

They wrap their tongues around the grass in the pasture, or the hay or silage in the feed bunk and bite it off with their lower incisors and the dental pad in their upper jaw. They chew it a bit with their molar teeth before swallowing the food. Later they will regurgitate their cud, and chew it more. A bovine has no upper incisors, only a hard dental pad.

So, if they happen to pick up a bit of scrap metal with their grass or hay, and chew very little before swallowing, it is easy to see how they get "hardware" in their stomachs.

The reticulum, or second part of the stomach, has a mucous lining that is deep and like a honeycomb. Once the bits of metal get into the reticulum, they are trapped, and just lie there. If there are enough to severely irritate the animal's stomach lining, the animal's appetite diminishes, and weight loss ensues. With the diminished appetite and the weight loss, the cow's milk production goes down. That is when the owner notices, because if the animal does not produce enough milk, he does not make money.

In a severe case of "hardware" disease, a sharp object such as a piece of fence wire, a long screw or nail will penetrate the wall of the reticulum and the diaphragm and enter the lungs. This generally is fatal to the cow because of an infection that occurs.

There are magnets available that can be given to a cow so that any metal object that is swallowed will attach to the magnet in the reticulum.

The magnet is simply inserted far back in the cow's mouth with a pill gun, she swallows it and it goes from the rumen to the reticulum and stays there. You might say when this is done, the cow has been magnetized for life.

᠎᠎᠎

Once, I was presented with a small poodle that, according to the owner, had swallowed a fluffy cloth ponytail holder.

We took an x-ray of the dog's stomach, but it showed nothing, so I phoned the owner to give her that information. I explained to her that we would have to feed the dog barium and take another radiograph. The barium would show up white around the foreign body in the stomach. She okayed that because she was sure the dog had swallowed the thing.

One of my employees called me to the phone about that time. I went to the front of the hospital to speak with a client. I suppose I talked about three minutes before returning to the dog. Lo and behold, the dog had vomited, and there lay the cloth ponytail holder.

᠎᠎᠎

It wasn't unusual to be presented with a cat or dog with a fish hook caught in one of its paws, lips or tongue. The hook could easily be removed by pushing the hook and barbs all the way through the tissue and cutting through the shaft. If the animal was calm enough this could be done without anesthetizing the animal.

One time, though, a client showed up with a dog that had just swallowed a fishing lure and the fishing line was still protruding from the dog's mouth. I immediately phoned the small animal clinic at the University of Illinois to tell them I was sending the dog to them.

They successfully removed the lure through an endoscope.

~~~~~

One of my clients owned a white German Shepherd dog that was just plain mean. He didn't like me -- I'm not sure he liked anyone. Because he was so mean, I didn't care much for him either.

During office hours one afternoon, the owner and his ten year-old son, Mikey, walked in the door with the dog. Mikey wasn't mean, but he was very mischievous.

The owner sat down in one of the waiting room seats, and I could see the dog from behind the counter in the business area. One glimpse of the dog told me he was in big trouble.

Rex had lost several pounds, the outline of the bones of his lumbar spine was very visible, and his abdomen was enlarged. In addition, his hair coat was rough and his eyes sunken and dull. To me, he was the picture of a dog with advanced heartworm disease. Since the dog was receiving heartworm prevention tablets, I didn't see how this could be possible. Sometimes, even though their intentions were good, owners would forget to give the daily dose of preventive medicine to their dog.

As Steve, the owner, led the dog slowly into my examining room, I marveled at how docile the dog was. He had yet to growl at me. Steve gingerly lifted the dog the twelve inches up to my examining table/scale. Immediately, the scale showed that the dog had lost twenty pounds since his last visit.

Steve held tightly to the dog's collar as I raised the hydraulic table to working height. I then checked his temperature which was slightly sub-normal. The dog was so depressed he didn't even growl at me when I used my stethoscope to listen to his heart and lungs. When I grasped some of his skin between my thumb and forefinger and lifted, the skin continued to stand when I released it. This dog was severely dehydrated.

Next I placed my hands on either side his abdomen. I didn't have to push to determine that his abdomen felt like one big rock.

I told the owner, "We need to take an x-ray to determine what's going on inside his stomach." The owner agreed, so I took him to the x-ray room. He was so docile, I decided we could take the x-rays without sedating him.

We placed the dog on his back and took the first x-ray. Then we rolled him onto his side and took a lateral view.

When I viewed the developed x-rays, I was amazed at what I saw. When I had palpated the abdomen, I thought that it felt like there was one big rock in his stomach.

No!! It was many smaller rocks!!!

The dog was still on the x-ray table with one of my female assistants in charge of him. He had always liked her, so I felt he would be all right. I went to the owner in the waiting room to tell him what I had found. I asked, "How would this dog get a stomach full of rocks?" "Mischievous Mikey" piped up with, "Oh, I throw driveway rocks into the air, and he catches and swallows them."

I explained to Steve that we needed to keep the dog because I intended to start intravenous fluids immediately. I needed to partially rehydrate him before I surgically removed the rocks. I also told Steve we would be giving the dog intravenous fluids during and after surgery the next day.

I performed the surgery the next morning and removed a one pound coffee can of white driveway rocks from the dog's stomach. Recovery was uneventful -- by the afternoon, the dog was sitting up in his cage. When we left the hospital that afternoon, the dog was alert, so we placed some drinking water in his cage. He needed all the fluids he could get to replace what he had lost. He had actually drawn water from his body tissues to try to help move those rocks out of his stomach.

The following morning, we noticed he had consumed all the water we had left in his cage. He was standing up, and when I walked into the cage room, he growled. I thought, "He must be feeling better." I instructed one of my assistants to feed him a small amount of soft food, which he ate immediately. We discharged the dog that afternoon with the instruction to "take the rocks out of his daily diet."

❧❧❧❧

Another challenging case was presented to me in the form of an eighty pound yellow Labrador male that had lost thirty pounds over a six weeks period while another veterinarian had been treating him for a "sore" throat. Eighty pounds had been his starting weight -- he weighed fifty when he was brought to me. The diagnosis of a sore throat was based on the fact the dog persistently vomited and wouldn't eat.

We hospitalized the dog but before the owner left the office, we took and developed an x-ray of the abdominal area. When we put the x-ray on the viewer, I immediately saw why the dog was vomiting. In the stomach, we saw a round object that could only be a ball, although we didn't know what kind.

I informed the owner there was no reason to observe the dog because we had found a ball in the dog's stomach. I also told her that we would give the dog some intravenous fluids and do surgery the following morning. Since this was a very gentle dog, I had no worries that he would bite my assistant as she oversaw the I.V. treatment.

The following morning's surgery was routine. The ball we found in the stomach of the dog was a rubber ball that one finds attached to a paddle with a rubber band. Due to the action of the gastric juices on it, the ball had turned black and was as hard as a rock.

The dog was discharged the following day. When he was returned the following week for suture removal, he had gained back eleven of those thirty pounds he had lost.

❧❧❧❧

I was called to a Purebred Angus Farm to treat a constipated cow. When I saw her, I assumed she had overeaten on corn. It's the policy of most farmers with beef cattle breeding herds to turn them into corn fields after the corn has been harvested. The cattle pick up some ears of corn that have been missed by the combine. I erroneously thought she had found a large amount of corn and overeaten.

We moved the cow into a stanchion (head gate) to hold her while I treated her. I passed my stomach tube and pumped a gallon of mineral oil into her stomach. With this gentle treatment, I hoped to move the obstructive substance out of the stomach and through the intestines. The cow was pregnant, and harsher treatment might cause her to abort her calf.

The following morning I returned to find that the cow still had not passed any feces.

Apparently the mineral oil wasn't going to solve the problem, so I decided to use a more powerful laxative. I informed the owner of my decision and told him that we might abort the calf. He said that the cow was more important than the calf. She could always have another calf next year if we successfully treated her now.

For this treatment, I mixed a powdered laxative and some warm water and pumped it into her stomach through the stomach tube.

When I returned the following morning, the cow still had not moved her bowels--but she had aborted the calf.

I was becoming perplexed by this time. Although there was no rumen movement, there was no bloating by the cow. I was beginning to think the cow might have eaten a piece of plastic that had blown into the field, and it was obstructing the movement of the food into the small intestine.

I conveyed these thoughts to the owner, and asked if he would be willing to let me open up the cow's stomach to determine what was the problem. This surgery is called a rumenotomy. He readily agreed because he wanted to save the cow.

It was Saturday morning, and I held walk-in hours for small animals from ten to twelve o'clock. I explained the situation to him and promised to return about one thirty p. m. to do the surgery. Since the cow was at the "other farm" and there was no house there, I asked him to bring me some warm water at that time.

After holding office hours, I went home for lunch. Our youngest son, Jim, was home from Culver Military Academy for the weekend, so I asked him to go along to help me with the surgery. He was excellent help, whether it was with large or small animal surgery.

I gave the cow a light dose of tranquilizer, clipped and prepped the left side of her abdomen and disinfected it prior to running a line block through the skin and muscle to provide anesthesia for the surgery. After disinfecting the skin, I anesthetized the line of the surgical incision and covered the area with a drape with a long slit in it. Working through the slit in the drape, I incised the cow's skin, muscle and peritoneum (the lining of the abdominal cavity).

I reached in and grasped the wall of the rumen to bring it outside the skin so I could make an incision. After making my incision in the stomach, I clamped the stomach wall to the drape so that none of the contents of the rumen would fall into the abdominal cavity.

It was imperative that we not contaminate, in any way, the area inside the body wall. If we did, we could end up with peritonitis, an infection of the lining of the abdominal cavity. Remember, we weren't doing surgery in the sterile environment of a human hospital surgical suite...we were working in a barn with dust on the rafters and cobwebs hanging from the ceiling.

Both my hands and arms were covered with plastic obstetrical gloves that were shoulder length, and I would need them as I intended to empty the rumen and reticulum of whatever was in the stomach.

Sitting on the floor of the barn near the cow were two five gallon buckets that were to be the receptacles for the stomach contents I was about to remove.

Jim was holding the clamps while I was using both hands to empty the stomach.

Before I had finished, I had filled both buckets with corn stalks and corn shucks, nothing but corn stalks and corn shucks. The cow had engorged herself with corn stalks and shucks to the point her digestive system had shut down, and she could not get any of the contents out of the stomach. The remainder of the ingesta I threw on the floor of the barn. I had totally emptied the cow's stomachs and had not found anything that would be blocking the movement of her stomach contents. To say the least, I was disappointed.

I closed the four incisions with four separate suture lines, and we cleaned up my equipment.

As we were driving home, I said to Jim, "I really blew it; I would have bet there was something in the third stomach that was impeding the flow of ingesta through the digestive tract."

When I returned the next morning to check on the cow, I couldn't believe my eyes.

The owner had given the cow hay, grain and water. She had drunk all the water, ate the grain, chewed on some of the hay, and lay there chewing her cud. Her digestive tract was functioning again.

Sometimes, veterinary medicine is just plain luck.

❧❧❧

I once had a call from a dog owner whose dog had chewed on a stick of dynamite.

Never having been faced with such a situation, the only advice was for the owner to give the dog a bowl of milk and keep him away from an open flame.

❧❧❧

I know of one dog that drank from the toilet stool with Sani Flush in the water, and another dog that chewed on a razor blade. Both dogs survived.

CHAPTER **20**

Dehorning Cattle

The job I disliked most in practicing veterinary medicine was dehorning cattle.

Farmers requested that their cattle be dehorned for various reasons. Beef cattle in a feedlot were dehorned to keep them from bruising the meat when they butted one another. Dairy cattle were not dehorned as often. However, if one cow tried to dominate the others by butting them, the farmer might decide to have her horns removed.

Dehorning was usually done outside, not in the barn. Sometimes the barn lots were muddy with manure lying around in piles. The job of dehorning was a bloody one. That's why I have always said that I went to veterinary school to work in the mud, the manure, and the blood.

Blocking of the cornual nerve with a local anesthesia would alleviate most of the pain associated with dehorning.

After the horn was removed, the cornual arteries could be grasped with a hemostat. Twisting of the hemostat stretched the artery until it broke. The broken end of the artery then recoiled into the bone of the skull and caused the blood to clot.

As I drove into the barnyard of Art Sandstrom, I could see that many of the dairy cows in the cow lot were shaking their heads.

Art met me as I got out of my car and I asked, "What's wrong with your cows, Art?"

"I'm dehorning them," he said.

"You're what?"

"Yah, I put those rubber bands that you use to castrate calves and lambs around their horns so the horns will fall off."

"That's not going to work, Art," I told him.

"Why not?"

"Calves' and lambs' scrotums are soft tissue, so when the stretched rubber bands contract, they shut off the circulation and the lower half of the scrotum and the testicles shrivel up and drop off."

"Why won't that work on the horns?"

"Because the horns are not soft tissue, they're hard tissue, and the rubber bands will not cut through hard tissue. After so long a time, the bands will break and fall off."

Fast forward a month and I was called to Art's farm remove a retained placenta from one of the Holstein dairy cows.

Art said, "You were right, Doc, those rubber bands fell off without taking the horns off. They did leave a little mark around the horn though."

♪♪♪♪

"Did you bring your horn saw?" asked Carl East when I got out of my car. I had gone to the East farm to dehorn three or four beef cows.

"No, am I going to need it?" I asked. I did have all the dehorning instruments I would need for any problem I might face. Mr. East was an older man and he liked to kid around, so I thought I would do some kidding of my own. "You sure are," he answered. "I've got a cow with a horn growing into her head and you'll need a saw to remove it."

"We'll see," I said.

I backed my cattle catch chute up to the door he indicated and unhitched my practice truck. As I operated the hydraulic jack to lower the chute to sit flat on the ground, I could hear him telling the neighbors who were helping that I was sure going to need a saw to remove that horn.

A cattle chute or catch chute or squeeze chute is pulled behind a vehicle to the farm destination, unhitched from the vehicle and lowered with a hydraulic jack to sit flat on the ground. The front end of the chute is actually a stanchion that, after the head of the animal passes through, can be closed on the neck to restrain the animal. The animal can freely move its head, but can't back up or go forward.

I dehorned three old cows by using the large guillotine type dehorners and all went smoothly. After the horn is removed with the dehorner, it is necessary to stop the bleeding from where the horn was removed. This is done by grasping the blood vessel with a small hemostat and twisting until the vein breaks and rolls up inside the bone.

Then, the cow with the horn growing toward the head entered the chute. I placed the head bar over her neck, and the bar over her nose to restrain her.

Taking a short piece of woven obstetrical wire with handles attached out of the back pocket of my coveralls, I slipped it between the horn and the head and started to saw the base of the horn with it. About that time Mr. East came out of another door in the barn, still talking about my need for a saw. Just as he walked up to me, the horn fell to the ground.

"Where's your saw?" he asked.

I showed him the obstetrical wire and said, "Right here."

I picked up my Keystone dehorners to remove the second horn, but Mr. East stopped me and said, "We'll just leave the other horn alone." I never figured out why he had me dehorn the other cows but left one horn on this cow.

꒰꒱

Another time, I was dehorning some six hundred pound Hereford heifers for Will Alison and his son Jake. After Jake walked in front of the chute twice as I was placing the head and nose bars on a heifer, I politely asked him not to do that.

When we had the next heifer secured in the cattle chute, I reached for the near end of the head bar which was lying on the ground. Just as I did so, Jake walked in front of the chute. The heifer, on her knees with her chin on the ground, jumped up and caught the head bar with her nose. The head bar flew out of my grasp and hit me in the mouth.

I know there are probably situations more painful than having a two inch square iron bar propelled by the head of a lunging six hundred pound heifer hit one in the mouth.

However, at the time, I don't believe I could have thought of one.

I swore under my breath that this would be the last time I would ever dehorn cattle, but I left my cattle chute at the Alison farm, knowing I would go back and finish the job.

Will Alison drove me to the doctor's office in my vehicle. On the way, I called my wife on the two way radio to tell her what had happened and asked her to meet me at the doctor's office. This wasn't the first time I had called her after being injured on the job.

In my truck on the way to the doctor's, I removed the bloody handkerchief from in front of my mouth and asked Will Alison, "How does it look?"

He replied, "I don't know, Doc, it makes me sick to look at it."

I found out from my doctor that my upper lip had a gash in it and that was where part of the blood was coming from; the rest was from my two upper middle incisor teeth. The left one had been loosened and moved to the left while the right tooth had been loosened and moved to the left behind the left incisor.

After the doctor had sutured my lip, he said, "You know, Al, I think you or I could put those teeth back where they belong." My reply was, "I'm not going to try, and I don't think I will let you, either. I'm going to my dentist." He just chuckled when I said that.

The fifteen mile trip to my dentist resulted in him restoring the teeth to their normal position and holding them in place with bonding. I admit I ate soft food for a few days, and never again did I take a bite of an apple with those incisors. They were good for about ten years before being replaced by dentures.

And yes, I did return to dehorn the rest of the heifers and, yes, I did continue to dehorn cattle after that accident.

ᴦᴦᴦᴦ

When I take my automobile to the mechanic, I might tell him what I think is wrong with it, but I do not try to tell him how to repair it. Likewise, when I go to the barber, I tell him how I like my hair to look, but I don't instruct him on how to cut it.

So when I get a client who is a successful businessman and is able to purchase a farm and the cattle to stock that farm, I don't take that client very seriously when he tries to tell me how to treat his livestock.

I do, however, like to joke around with that particular type of client.

When the hired man and I were dehorning some aged Hereford cows and the owner showed up in yellow trousers and a pastel green shirt straight from the golf course, I just knew that I had to somehow get a little blood on those fancy clothes. In addition, he had his banker with him, and I would have been doubly happy to spot his clothes a little with blood as well.

Try as I might, I couldn't lure them in close enough to get a little splatter on them. As these were old cows and their bones were probably brittle, I was using obstetrical wire to saw off the horns. The sawing motion creates heat and cauterizes the blood vessel, and the blood doesn't squirt as far as it would with a guillotine type dehorner.

The next day I did place a pair of those horns, with a lariat wrapped around them, on the hood of his car at the restaurant where we drank our early morning coffee.

ᴦᴦᴦᴦ

I was called by a dairy farmer to dehorn an aged Holstein cow and, as I got out of my truck with my nose lead in one hand and some obstetrical wire in the other, he asked, "Where are your dehorners?"

I replied, "I don't want to use them, I might crack her skull."

"I'll bet you're not strong enough to use the big dehorners on this old cow."

Willard Carp was the farmer's name. Everything about Willard was big… voice, mouth, beer belly, laugh, and ideas.

I returned to my truck and took out my Keystone dehorners. Those dehorners were about four feet long and had guillotine type blades. When the handles were open, the blades were apart. After placing the blades over the horn and next to the head, the handles were closed. Admittedly, it took all the strength I had to close the blades and sever the horn from the head.

We entered the barn and I walked in front of the stanchions to the cow. I placed my nose lead in the cow's nasal septum and pulled her head to the left, wrapped the rope over the top of the stanchion and handed the end to Willard to hold.

After I had blocked the cornual nerves I placed the opened blades over the first horn and steadily closed the handles, removing the first horn. Then I repeated the procedure on the other horn. As the second horn fell to the floor, I accidentally dropped my dehorner, blade end first, and it hit the concrete with a bang. When I looked at the blades, I could see the bottom blade was split.

"Look at this, Willard, that horn was so hard it split my dehorner blade. And you didn't think I was strong enough to use these dehorners. I was so strong, I split the blade."

Actually, I thought the blade split when it fell and hit the concrete, but I wanted him to believe I caused the split because of my strength.

CHAPTER 21

The Gates Family

For the past few summers our grandson, Dalton, and I have been picking wild raspberries in a timber about fifteen miles from where we live. He likes raspberries almost as much as I do. I developed a taste when my parents had large patches of strawberries and black raspberries when I was growing up. I didn't mind picking raspberries, but strawberries were another matter, so I usually talked my older sisters into picking them. I guess I like raspberries so much because my mother baked the tastiest pie that I have ever eaten.

Coming home from one such excursion, Dalton noticed an old ramshackle barn along the road, and he said, "Grandpa, I think if another board came off of that barn, it would collapse." I agreed with him and then told him about the barn on the Gates farm.

I mentioned that his grandmother went with me one night to deliver a calf for Joe Gates. After a successful delivery, and as we were walking out of the barn, my wife whispered to me, "What holds this barn up?" I whispered back, "I don't know, but if you noticed, I didn't tie the cow to the barn, but to a post in the center of the pen."

After I had told this story to Dalton, he replied, "No offense, Grandpa, but I can't envision Grandma going on farm calls with you."

In fact, my wife often went on emergency night farm calls after our three children were grown and away at school.

The Gates barn was an ordinary barn with lean-tos built on either end. I suspect that the lean-to on the east end of the barn was what kept the barn from falling over. The barn was leaning so far to the east that the doors on the south side lacked being able to be closed by about six inches.

My first association with Joe Gates came soon after I opened my practice when my phone rang one morning. I hadn't had too many requests for my services yet, so I was thrilled each time the phone rang. Such was the case when I answered it one morning, and the caller said, "This is Joe Gates" followed by the question, "Are you busy this morning?" As much as I would have liked to be able to tell him I was covered up, I had to answer truthfully and tell him no and ask what he needed.

He replied that his son's high school agriculture class was coming out to his farm that morning, and the teacher was going to "fix some busted pigs," and he would like to have me there in case he ran into trouble. Fixing "busted pigs," in farmer terms means castrating pigs and repairing inguinal hernias while doing so. The problem is that some loops of the small intestine have slipped from the abdomen through the inguinal canal and have dropped into the sac of the testicle. The same problem occurs in humans, but the surgical repair in humans is usually more complicated. Mainly because castration isn't part of inguinal hernia repair in the human.

In pigs, the procedure for performing this surgery is to have a person hold the pig by the rear legs with his head down while the holder applies pressure to the pig's body with his knees.

During the hernial repair, the pig's testicles are removed and the enlarged inguinal ring through which the intestines descended is sutured closed. The incision in the skin is closed with sutures to complete the surgery.

This is the procedure that has been used in our country for generations, and may seem cruel, but seems to affect the pigs very little. They go right back to the feed trough without showing any evidence of pain. This is done when the pigs are around thirty pounds, or less, in weight. Some farmers perform this procedure themselves, but instead of suturing the incision, close it with rings normally placed in pigs' noses to keep them from rooting.

In England, they are required to administer an anesthetic, but the pigs they are castrating are much larger. Before long, anesthesia may be required in this country when such surgery is performed.

The Gates farm was not far from where we lived, but the last part of the trip was very pretty as the road paralleled the river for a few hundred yards. In later years, I always looked for the head of a Canadian goose sitting on her nest in the top of a hollow tree.

When I arrived at the farm, the agriculture class, consisting of about six students and the teacher, were already there. After Joe introduced me, I suggested the instructor start on the first pig, telling him I would help if he had problems with the surgery.

He replied that he hadn't done this in a while, and perhaps I should do the first pig so he could refresh his memory about the surgical procedure.

Although I was taught how to perform this particular surgery in veterinary college, I really became proficient when I interned with Dr. Bob Strahler at Abingdon, Illinois, during the summer between my third and fourth years of veterinary school. Dr. Strahler was very patient with me, and I developed many of my surgical techniques while working with him. Although a general practitioner, Dr. Strahler provided veterinary service to many farmers who raised swine.

I have to admit that I was trying to impress Joe Gates, the farmer, so he would want to become a client of mine. However, I also wanted to show the teacher that I was much more qualified to perform such surgery than he.

I don't know if I impressed Mr. Gates, but I must have impressed the teacher because when I finished the surgery on the pig, I turned to him and said, "Okay, it's your turn now." He replied, "I think you better do the rest of them, Doc."

This was the beginning of a client/doctor relationship with one of my favorite clients and lasted until Joe passed away, and after that with his son Rick, until my retirement thirty-nine years later. For some reason unknown to me, Joe never called me Doctor or "Doc," but called me "Professor."

Joe once told me about a bred (pregnant) cow he had bought and was hoping would produce a male calf that would become his herd bull.

As I was eating lunch not long after that, the phone rang and it was Joe. "Doc, that cow I told you about is calving and she's having trouble." "Okay, I'll be right out," I replied.

Long before this, we had moved into town, so it would take longer to get to the Gates farm. I left half my lunch uneaten and jumped into my practice vehicle and probably broke some speed limits in my haste to deliver the calf that was so important to Joe.

Since Joe always joked with me, when I arrived at his place, I said with a deadpan face, "If I deliver a live calf, I expect to be half owner," and Joe laughingly agreed.

As I examined the cow, I could see the feet of the calf emerging from the vulva, and the nostrils of the calf could also be seen if I spread the lips of the vulva. I determined that I would try to deliver the calf without using my fetal extractor, so I placed my nylon obstetrical straps around the calf's feet above the ankles. Then I sat down behind the cow who was lying on her side, placed my feet against her upper legs with my knees bent and, as I pulled, straightened my legs. The calf began to emerge from the birth canal, and when his hips popped through the pelvic inlet, the calf came with a rush, and I fell back against the bucket of warm water Joe had brought for me to use to clean up after I finished with my work. Although I was somewhat damp from the water, I was happy to see the calf was alive. When Joe saw the calf breathing, he said, "Now I'll have a really good herd bull in a couple of years."

I learned later that the next noon when Joe went in for lunch, he said to his wife, "I can't find my utility tractor. I wonder who came and borrowed it." It was the policy that if a neighbor needed a piece of machinery he would borrow it from another neighbor, even if the person was not at home.

Mrs. Gates asked, "Joe weren't you driving the tractor when you found that cow in the timber yesterday morning?"

He replied, "By golly, I was."

After lunch, Joe walked out in the timber and found the tractor with the engine still running.

Through the years I delivered many calves and pigs, but one other calving case still sticks in my mind. Apparently Joe had not checked on his beef cow herd for a couple of days, and when he did he found a cow in labor. It appeared that she could not get up on her feet, so Joe rounded up three or four neighbors and they somehow loaded her onto a tilt bed, two wheel trailer which he pulled up to the barn with a tractor.

When I arrived, the trailer was backed up to the open end of a lean-to shed attached to the barn, and Joe and the neighbors were standing there laughing and joking around. I took my calving equipment out of my vehicle and carried it over to the trailer. With my obstetrical straps around the lower legs of the calf, I positioned my fetal extractor in position at the rump of the cow. (A fetal extractor, commonly called a calf puller is a long metal rod with a U shaped end that fits around the cow's rump. On the other end is a winch with a wire cable attached. On the end of the cable is a hook that can be used to grasp the obstetrical straps. When the handle of the winch is worked back and forth, the cable is would around a spool, and in this manner the calf is slowly brought out of the birth canal).

This was one of the easiest calf deliveries I did in nearly forty years of practice. I didn't even have to get on my knees to place the straps on the calf's legs. Since the cow was on a trailer bed which was about three feet high, I could stand and do the work. As I began to operate the fetal extractor to deliver the calf, I could see that the calf was dead.

This was to be expected since the cow had obviously been in labor for several hours or more.

Joe and the neighbors who were helping him slowly slid the cow off the tilted trailer and into the west lean-to of the barn and closed the gate.

Joe said, "I bet she hasn't had a drink for quite some time," and went to get a pail of fresh water.

When he returned, he climbed over the gate into the pen with the water. His feet had no sooner hit the ground, than the cow jumped up and chased him out of the pen.

We all laughed, and one of the men said, "Joe, I think you just set a world record for climbing over a six foot gate."

I guess the cow wasn't as worn out as I thought from her several hours of labor.

Often, Joe could be quite a practical joker. One time my parents were visiting us and my Dad went with me to Joe's to treat a sick calf. Joe always kept a grain wagon just inside the door of the barn. He kept ground feed in the wagon to feed the animals who were in pens in the barn.

As we were walking toward the door on our way out after treating the calf, Joe said, "If you can catch that rooster, you can have him." I looked up and saw a rooster weighing about three pounds perched on the wagon box. I had played a lot of softball and baseball when I was younger and I have to admit, I had quick hands. Without looking at the bird, I quickly reached up and grabbed him by the legs with my right hand. I believe I surprised Joe with my quickness.

I said, "Joe, get a gunny sack (burlap bag)." Joe was laughing when he returned.

My Dad held the chicken in the burlap bag as I drove home. When we arrived at our house, there was still time for Dad to kill and prepare the chicken for Mary Jane to fry for our lunch. As I took my first bite of chicken, I realized why Joe had been laughing when he brought the gunny sack to me. That was the toughest chicken I have ever tried to chew.

Joe passed away several years ago, but wherever he is today, he is probably still laughing about that chicken.

One morning I stopped at a local restaurant for a cup of coffee, and one of the other patrons called to me, saying, "Hey, Doc, I want to ask you a question." This wasn't unusual, for people often asked me for free advice about their animals.

When I walked up to the table where the questioner was sitting, he showed me two walnuts and asked, "How can I find out how old these walnuts are?"

I said, "They look to me like they just fell off the tree."

"No, no, they're old and perfectly preserved. I'm drilling a well out at Joe Gates' farm, and these two walnuts came to the surface from way down in the earth."

I said, "I guess you could take them down to the National History Survey people at the University of Illinois and see if they can carbon date them."

I suspected what had happened. Somehow and sometime after the first day's drilling, Joe had gotten the walnuts down the well shaft so that the driller would bring them to the surface on the second day.

I saw Joe a day or two later and asked him how he got the walnuts down the shaft and he just laughed. A few days later, I saw the well driller and asked him if he had found out how old the walnuts were and he said, "Aww, Doc, you know what happened."

Two or three of Joe's nephews were also farmers in the area. One of them, Beryl, was pretty squeamish when he saw blood.

One morning, Beryl brought a small calf with a compound fracture of the lower right front leg into my hospital for treatment. The fracture was of several days duration and was infected. I explained the problem to Beryl and told him the only way to save the calf was to amputate the lower leg. I also warned him that when the calf attained about six hundred pounds in body weight, he would need to slaughter him because supporting all that weight on one foreleg would cause the leg to bow drastically. Eventually, the one foreleg would not be able to support the weight of the calf.

Beryl agreed to have the calf's leg amputated, but he allowed that he would have to wait in his pickup truck while I did the surgery. I had just started the surgical procedure when the bell on the door of my waiting room chimed. I didn't need to ask who it was because immediately I heard the voice of Joe Gates asking, "Anyone here?" I replied that I was in the surgery room. Shortly, Joe and his son Rick walked into the surgery room.

"Why is Beryl sitting outside in his pickup?" Joe asked.

I explained that I was going to amputate the lower portion of the calf's leg and he didn't feel he was up to watching the surgery.

"Sounds like Beryl," said Joe, laughing.

I had already given the calf a dose of tranquilizer and had done a ring block with procaine anesthetic around the calf's leg and was clipping the hair preparatory to scrubbing and disinfecting the skin when Joe and Rick walked in. "Mind if we watch?" asked Joe. I wasn't concerned about either of them getting sick or fainting on me, so I said, "Okay. "

The procedure for what I was planning to do required making an incision entirely around the leg about two inches below the knee. The knee in the calf is comparable to the wrist of a human. The skin is then reflected upward before removing the lower leg at the knee joint. This is necessary to have skin over the end of upper bone.

As I was suturing the wound resulting from the amputation, Joe asked, "What are you going to do with the part of the leg that you cut off?"

I said, laughingly, "Give to you for a soup bone, if you want it."

"Just watch what I do with it," Joe said, with a big smile.

I finished bandaging the stump of the leg, and Joe grabbed the amputated part of the leg, and he and Rick started for the back door. I followed him to see what he was going to do. Beryl had been sitting in his pickup truck with the driver's side window rolled down about four inches all the while I was doing surgery on the calf. Joe walked up to the passenger side door of the pickup, opened it, and tossed the amputated leg on the passenger seat. I thought Beryl was going to try to climb out the space between the top of the door and the partially rolled down window. Joe and Rick just stood there and laughed.

On another occasion, Beryl phoned me and asked me to come to his farm to "look" at a cow that wasn't doing very well.

On arrival at his farm I found an Angus cow that truly "wasn't doing very well." She was lying down in the barn lot and had been for a while, judging from the way the soil was packed under and around her. She obviously had lost some weight, and her hair coat looked rough like she was having a "bad hair day."

I went through my usual routine of examining an animal. Her temperature was normal, and her rumen movements were diminished, although she showed evidence of diarrhea. Her gums were pale and blood vessels in the whites of her eyes were almost non-existent.

Beryl asked, "What do you think is wrong with her, Doc?" I responded, "Beryl, she's starving." I thought he was going to cry when he said, "That's a heck of a thing to say to a man, that he's starving his cow to death."

I replied, "Beryl, I didn't say you were starving this cow. She's starving because she has so many stomach worms, she can't take advantage of the food she has been eating."

I treated the cow with intravenous fluids, and injected some vitamins intramuscularly. Lastly, I injected her with a good dose of worm medicine subcutaneously to kill the worms. Then I suggested that we treat all the cows to kill any worms they might have. However, Beryl opted not to do so. A day or two later, Beryl came into my office to tell me the cow was up and eating.

Thereafter, when he saw a cow that had a rough hair coat or "didn't look right," he came to my office to get a "shot of that good worm medicine" so he could treat the cow.

Beryl had a brother named Leonard who also called on me to treat his livestock.

One morning, he phoned me to tell me that one of his cows had given birth to a calf with only three legs. Excitedly, he told me he had gone to the barn to check his cows since it was calving time, and he had seen the newborn calf lying in the straw. He said when he had tried to get the calf to stand, he saw it was missing one front leg. The skin of the shoulder was smooth and covered with hair.

. "Have you ever heard of such a thing, Doc?" he asked. I told him that I had seen a calf born with the knees and ankles of both front legs bending the wrong way so that the calf would have walked on the top of his hooves had he been alive. I told him, also, that I had delivered a dead lamb that had eight legs and two heads.

Leonard was a fun loving guy -- always wanting to bet about something or match coins for a cup of coffee or anything else that came across his mind.

He was a tenant farmer, and in addition to growing crops, he and the farm owner had a herd of Angus cattle. Leonard provided the labor to raise the crops and take care of the cattle, while the landowner provided the land and the buildings to house the cattle. They shared the expenses and the profits equally.

Leonard also owned a farm down the road where he raised swine.

Readers of this book are probably wondering why I am telling you all this, but what you have just read leads up to the next part of the story.

I was called out one Sunday to treat a sick cow co-owned by Leonard and the landowner, Mr. Lockwood. However, the cow wasn't at the farm where Leonard lived.

He and Mr. Lockwood had rented some pasture a couple of miles away, and that was where I went to see the cow.

After treating the cow (I don't remember what was wrong with her), I presented Leonard with a bill for twelve dollars. Remember, this was in the 1970's. He immediately said, "Match you double or nothing," and for once I agreed to match with him. We matched and I won, so now Leonard owed me twenty-four dollars. He immediately said, "Charge half of that to Joe Lockwood." So, I did.

Two or three days later, Joe Lockwood came into my office and said, "I need to look at your books." I replied, "The only people entitled to look at my books are my wife and the IRS."

"Why do you think you need to see them? " I asked.

"I think Gates is cheating me," Joe replied, I told him that I knew Leonard wasn't cheating because I billed each of them equally for any treatments I did on the cattle, and when I treated Leonard's hogs

I billed those charges one hundred percent to him. I didn't tell him that he was paying six dollars to me because Leonard lost when we matched double or nothing.

Mr. Lockwood was a lot older than I and a very wealthy man, but I said to him, "If you don't trust the man, get rid of him as a tenant."

Interestingly enough, Joe Lockwood later told Leonard about the advice I had given him and was laughing when he told him. I guess he thought a young man such as I, struggling to get ahead in the world, had a lot of nerve giving a wealthy man like him advice.

CHAPTER 22

Hanging Out

Medical dictionaries define uterine prolapse as the falling or sliding of the uterus (womb) from its normal position into the vaginal area.

In animals, prolapse of the uterus goes one step further and falls out of the body to hang under the tail like a big cylindrical tube in the cow or sow, or a balloon in the case of the horse.

The cow, dairy or beef, seems more prone to prolapse or evert their uterus immediately after giving birth to their young than any other animal. However, other species of animals evert their wombs as well.

A prolapsed uterus is nothing but the uterus turned wrong side out just as you would turn one of your socks wrong side out.

If the cow has a difficult time giving birth to her calf, or her rear end is lower than her head (she is lying with her rear end downhill), she is more likely to continue to strain after the calf is born. Continued straining causes the uterus to push through the vaginal tract with the inside of the uterus showing on the outside. Although I had been taught what the lining of a bovine uterus looked like, and I had felt the inside of a uterus, I never could grasp such a fact until I saw my first prolapsed uterus in a cow. There, looking right at me were the caruncles to which the cotyledons of the cow's placenta attach. The caruncles looked like a bunch of strawberries glued to the lining of the uterus. It is the caruncles from which the cotyledons of the placenta have to be detached to remove a retained placenta.

My first experience with a uterine prolapse came during the summer I was interning with Dr. Strahler after my third year in veterinary college. The Strahlers were out for the evening, and somehow the farmer got the telephone number to the apartment where we were living.

When he called and told me his problem, I told him I would be out in a short time, never doubting that I was capable of replacing a uterus in a cow. Such is the confidence of youth. Since I had never seen a uterine prolapse, I guess I was more confident in my abilities than I had a right to be.

The cow was out in the middle of a large pasture when I arrived with no place to tie her. The farmer assured me that once I put a rope on her, he could hold her so that she would not move and, gullible me, I believed him.

I knew that I needed to inject a local anesthetic into the second caudal (tail) space to deaden the nerves and prevent her from straining when I attempted to replace the uterus. I readily completed that task, and while the anesthetic was taking effect, I began to cleanse and disinfect the uterus. After washing the organ with warm water and surgical soap with a small amount of disinfectant added, I rubbed white sugar into the mucosa (lining) of the uterus. Shortly, liquid began to drip from the swollen uterus. As the uterus is suspended through the vaginal opening, it is "squeezed" by the muscles of the vagina, causing a lack of blood flow back into the body, and the uterus becomes turgid or swollen. The sugar I placed on the uterine lining removed the fluid from the uterine wall by osmosis. Actually, I rubbed sugar into the lining of the uterus more than one time or until the uterus was soft and pliable. Before I began to replace the uterus, I rubbed mineral oil all over it to help make it slick so that it might go back through the vaginal tract easier.

So far, the cow had stood quietly, held by the farmer, while I had prepped her for replacing the uterus.

Replacing a prolapsed uterus in a cow has always seemed to me like placing a bushel of potatoes into a peck sack…there never seemed to be enough room. The uterus came out through the vagina, so it had to go back. Right?

After placing plastic obstetrical sleeves on my two hands and arms, I gently lifted the uterus and began working it back into the vagina. The cow took a couple of steps and what advantage I had gained was lost. This went on for about a half hour, and I was gaining nothing. Except, I was now about fifty feet away from my car. Contrary to his promise, the farmer could not keep the cow from moving.

Then, I had an inspiration. A friend of mine, who had just graduated in June, had a practice in a town about eleven miles away. So I suggested the farmer call him and ask if he would come out and give me a hand. The farmer seemed relieved when I suggested that we get some additional professional help. He wasn't any more relieved than I was when my friend drove up, however.

The first words out of my friend's mouth were, "Yep, had a case like this last week. Couldn't get it back in. Cut it off. She died the next day."

I thought to myself, *"Great, that's just what the farmer needed to hear."*

My friend asked me to place both my hands under the uterus and lift while he attempted to replace it. Then I realized that I would never have been able to replace the uterus. It would be almost physically impossible to hold the organ, weighing fifty pounds or more, with one hand while working it back into the vagina with the other.

Thanks to my newly graduated veterinarian friend, the uterus was replaced, we didn't have to cut it off, and the cow lived to produce more calves.

I vowed there would never be another instance where I would not be able to replace a prolapsed uterus, and there wasn't. The reason…I learned that I needed another pair of hands, sometimes two pairs, to do the job.

Sows sometimes evert their uterus, and when they do, it is almost impossible for me to replace one because of the length of the organ...possibly six feet. My arms are only thirty-two inches. Besides, the farmer usually finds the sow dead when he goes to the farrowing house in the morning after she has given birth to pigs the night before.

An elderly hog farmer phoned me on a Sunday evening with the news that he had a sow trying to "throw out her innards after having pigs." I asked him how much of the uterus was out and he said, "about a foot and a half."

"Do you think you can hold it in until I get there?" I asked.

"I'll try."

I jumped into my practice truck and took back roads for most of the fifteen miles to his place so that I could drive faster.

When I arrived, Gene was down on his knees with two hands full of sow uterus, but he hadn't allowed her to push any more out.

Fortunately, none of the uterus had touched the floor of the crate so it was as clean as it would have been inside the body.

With OB sleeves on both arms, I bathed the uterus in clean mineral oil and gently replaced it in the sow, and extended my right arm as far as I could. I fervently hoped that I had gotten the uterine horn far enough in so that the sow would not strain and throw it back out. After placing a sulfa bolus in the uterus, I sutured the lips of the vulva together with an x suture. I then gave the sow an injection of penicillin and an injection of oxytocin. The penicillin would protect the sow against infection and the oxytocin would cause the uterus to contract as well as let down her milk to feed the pigs.

I left instructions for the farmer to phone me if the sow wasn't eating the next morning and to remove the sutures from the vulva after three days. The next time I saw the farmer, he told me the sow had gotten along just fine.

ͻͻͻ

Early one icy winter morning, I received a call from one of my favorite clients. He wasn't a favorite client because he had so much work for me to do, but because his wife baked fabulous peanut butter cookies. If I had a scheduled call at Dick's farm, I always left time to have a cup of coffee and cookie that they invariably invited me in for.

This particular morning, his complaint was that "there was something hanging out of one of his ewes." It was lambing season, so I assumed it was placenta (afterbirth). I told him I could leave immediately for his farm.

As I drove the icy roads for the fifteen miles to Dick's farm, I thought about his livestock: a few beef cows, a few head of sheep, a couple of sows, and two burros.

I would never get rich doing his veterinary work but he spent a couple of hundred dollars per year with me. Besides, there was the added advantage of those delicious cookies.

As I drove into the farm yard, I could see Dick holding a string with something on the end of it.

When I got out of the car, he kind of swung the object on the end of the piece of hay baler twine and asked, "That's afterbirth, right?"

As much as I didn't want to, I had to say, "I'm sorry, no, Dick, that's uterus."

"Well, I put this loop of twine around it and tugged real gently, and it came right off."

He may have tugged gently, but when he tugged the loop tightened and the twine amputated the uterus.

"I'll suture the lining of her vagina together so that none of her other organs will come out, and in three days you can sell her for slaughter."

I was too early for coffee and cookies that morning, so I headed back to my animal hospital on those slippery country roads.

♪♪♪♪

I had always dreaded that one day I would receive a phone call telling me that I was needed to replace a prolapsed uterus in a horse. I had escaped such a call for thirty years, but it finally came…at two o'clock on a cold January morning.

"I'll be out right away," I groggily told Joe Roberts at Liberty Bell Farm. I was at this farm a lot because they bred about a hundred mares each year. In addition, I vaccinated all their mares, foals and racing stock.

I hadn't been too crazy about treating horses until Joe bought this farm and moved to the area. I had not had the opportunity to treat Standardbreds (harness horses) until that time. Compared to the Thoroughbreds (flat racers) I had been used to treating in the Large Animal Clinic at the University of Illinois, most of these horses were a joy to handle.

I also enjoyed treating the big draft horses, Belgians, Percherons, and even mules. It was the backyard horses that I didn't like to treat. Some of the owners had little knowledge about horses, and I always felt that if I were going to be injured while treating a horse, it would be a backyard horse.

As I neared the horse farm, I was still dreading having to replace a uterine prolapse in a horse. First of all, I couldn't give the horse an epidural anesthetic to keep her from straining as I attempted to replace the uterus. It was doubtful I could stand directly behind the horse to replace the uterus. Oh, yes I could, at the risk of getting kicked.

After gathering the equipment and supplies I would need from my truck, I walked into the alleyway of the barn. Joe and one of the grooms were down at the far end of the barn, so I headed that way.

As I neared the stall where they were standing, Joe said, "She's a mean one, Doc."

I walked up to the door of the stall and peered through the bars. The walls were solid wood about five feet up from the ground and one inch vertical pipes ran up for another four feet before being topped with 2" x 4" lumber.

The mare was lying on the floor of the stall, but she hadn't always been there. There was blood from the uterus smeared all around the walls of the stall. Joe repeated again, "She's a mean one, Doc." I didn't think he was trying to intimidate me, but if he was, it was working.

I decided it would be a good idea if I gave the mare a light dose of tranquilizer before attempting to treat her, so I told Joe I would be back shortly and headed to my truck for a syringe, needle and a bottle of acepromazine.

Loading my syringe as I was returning to the barn, I told Joe I would try to sneak into the stall and slip an injection into her jugular vein. An I.V. injection would take effect quicker than if I injected it intramuscularly.

As I quietly slid open the door to the stall, Joe said, "Be careful, Doc."

It took me about three steps to reach the mare, and I quickly bent over and slipped the needle into the jugular vein and injected the tranquilizer. The mare didn't bat an eye or move a muscle.

I waited about ten minutes and then asked Joe to get the mare to her feet. He walked in, attached the lead shank to the mare's halter, clucked twice and tugged on the lead rope. The horse immediately rose to her feet.

I opened the stall door wide and asked Joe to back the rear end of the horse into the open doorway. With the mare's posterior in the doorway, I could stand to the side behind the wall and reach over to the rear of the mare. As Joe got the horse's rear situated into the doorway, the groom returned with a bucket of warm water.

I squirted some liquid disinfectant and soap on the uterus which was a little larger than a basketball and much smoother than the uterus of a cow or sheep. The horse, like the sow, has a diffuse placenta which means the connections are spread over much of the uterus rather than many attachments as in ruminants, but the mare had already released the afterbirth.

Donning the obstetrical sleeves, I splashed water on the uterus and rubbed the soap around to cleanse the uterus. Then I carefully washed off all the soap. Following this, I rubbed mineral oil over all the surface, placed both hands under the uterus and lifted it above the level of the pelvic floor. With a big whoosh, the organ fell through the vaginal canal and into the abdominal cavity....what a relief!!

After placing a sulfa urea bolus into the uterus, I gave the mare injections of oxytocin and penicillin intramuscularly. The oxytocin would stimulate the mare to contract her uterus and lessen her chances of prolapsing again.

Joe then walked the mare across the alleyway to a clean stall and placed the foal with her. The foal immediately began to nurse. The foal's nursing would also stimulate the uterus to contract.

I thought to myself, *"Why did I dread an equine uterine prolapse? That was a snap."*

A year or so later another veterinarian and I were talking about various cases (one probably trying to outdo the other as to our prowess as a veterinarian). I mentioned I had treated my first equine uterine prolapse and proceeded to relate my experience. When I finished, he immediately said, "Bet she didn't breed back."

I was pleased to say, "As a matter of fact, she did...on the foal heat. What's more, she dropped a live foal eleven months later." So much for one-upmanship.

A horse exhibits estrus (heat) seven to fifteen days, usually about nine days, after foaling. Conception may occur if the mare is bred at this time. Foal heat is also referred to as ninth day heat.

❧❧❧

I have replaced prolapsed uteri in many strange places, once in bitter cold weather with the cow lying on ice that was too slick for her to be able to rise.

Probably the strangest place was in a pasture in a briar patch.

When I arrived at the farm after getting the call for a cow with a uterine prolapse, I asked the farmer the whereabouts of the cow.

"She's in the pasture," he replied. "Follow me."

He got into his pickup and I into my vehicle and we started out into the forty acre timber pasture. Presently, he stopped and there lay the cow in a patch of wild raspberry bushes. Not only that, but the protruding uterus looked like a red rubber tube about six inches in diameter and six feet long. I had never seen a uterus as stretched out as this one.

"I tried to get her into the barn, Doc, but all she wanted to do was run away from me. I must have chased her for an hour all over this pasture. Then, she finally lay down in the briar patch, all pooped out."

I thought to myself, "*That accounts for the stretched out uterus and the almost total exhaustion of the cow.*"

I was amazed the uterus was not severely torn, but upon examination it seemed to be in reasonably good shape but, like the cow, worn out.

I performed a caudal epidural spinal block to keep the cow from straining while I manipulated the uterus, prepped the cow and started to replace the uterus. An injection of oxytocin would serve to help the uterus contract, I hoped. Tearing open some clean paper bags that cattle feed had come in, I placed them under the uterus after I had washed it.

The uterus, being so stretched out, was very pliable. I started by inserting my plastic sleeve-covered arm into the opening of the uterus. Pushing and rolling the walls of the uterus inward, I could feel that I was making some headway. It was like rolling up one's sleeves. Only instead of rolling outwardly, I was rolling inwardly.

I kept thinking to myself, *"patience, patience,"* something I had often been told by my wife that I lacked.

Finally, the last of the uterus fell into place, or I should say I pushed it into place. After inserting two intrauterine sulfa urea boluses as far into the uterus as I could and giving the cow an injection of antibiotics, I administered a nine hundred cc bottle of electrolytes and glucose. This treatment, I hoped, would help the cow survive the trauma she had suffered. I then suggested that the farmer get her a bucket of fresh water to drink.

A phone call from the farmer the following morning told me that the cow was up at the barn and was eating hay.

CHAPTER **23**

Starvation Rations

My first introduction to a starving animal came early in my practice years. I was called to see a Shetland pony that was down and couldn't rise. The animal was thin and emaciated and was on the verge of death. As I looked around, I could see several other ponies that were nearly as thin as the one that was down.

I could also see that the pasture they were grazing on was chewed right down to the earth. As a friend of mine would have said, "The ponies were eating sand and spitting rocks."

I asked the owner if he was feeding his ponies anything besides the grass they were getting from the pasture, and he replied in the negative.

As I was preparing to administer intravenous fluids and vitamins, I explained to the owner what I was doing in an attempt to save his pony's life. I was honest with the owner, however, and told him I feared the pony was too near death to save.

I then suggested that he might want to buy some grain and hay to feed his other animals because they, like the down pony, were slowly starving to death from a lack of food. I mentioned that he should bring in a manure sample for me to check for worm eggs. Then, if I saw worm eggs under the microscope when I examined the feces, we should treat the ponies to rid them of their worms.

He never did bring in a fecal sample for examination, but he must have started giving the ponies hay and grain, because I could see as I drove by that they were gaining weight.

♪♪♪

I don't recall seeing starving cattle until the advent of the big, round bales of hay.

Whereas the small "square" (actually rectangular) bales of hay only weighed about forty to fifty pounds, the big, round bales weigh about six hundred pounds. The smaller bales were generally stored in a hay mow in the barn or other shed out of the weather where they were kept dry. Often, the big bales are left out in the field, sometimes wrapped in plastic, but not always. Many of the big bales become moldy in the center from lying out in the weather. This reduces the feed value of the hay.

If we are having a mild winter, the beef cows can usually get by on a diet of hay and, perhaps, some corn shucks that have been baled. There might be a few kernels of corn in the shucks that the combine missed.

However, if a real cold spell comes along and stays very long, the cattle need a source of carbohydrates and fat because they are using up their own fat to heat their bodies.

I once saw three cows that were down from starvation in an old shed with no windows, so it was as cold in the shed as outside. The owner had thrown some hay in front of each of the cows, but they weren't eating. It was obvious to me that these cows were so far gone that they were going to die.

Some of the cows outside the shed had their heads through the openings in the walls of the shed wanting the hay.

This was during a prolonged cold period. I asked the owner how many cows were in the herd and he said two hundred. "And how many bales of hay are you feeding per day?" I asked.

"Fifty," he responded.

"I think you need to up that to a hundred bales a day and feed them some grain as well."

He bristled up and said, "Hay is expensive."

Whereupon, I said, "So are dead cows, and you have three right here, and if you don't start feeding them better, you're going to have more."

The farmer was feeding the small square bales and the hay was good quality, but he just wasn't feeding enough.

❧❧❧❧

The most serious case of starvation in cattle occurred in a herd owned by a local businessman who first bought a farm and then started a beef cattle herd with cows he had purchased from various sources. Most of these cows were past their prime and had been foisted off on him by people who took advantage of him.

He knew very little about livestock and was the type of person who would ask advice from a half dozen people and heed none of it. Also, it was up to the hired help to take care of the cattle, and they were not experienced in cattle husbandry, either.

The first inkling I had of a cow starving was in December when I was called to treat a cow that was down in the barn. The cow was recumbent and could not even raise her head. I knew she had no chance of surviving.

I talked to the owner and explained it was cold and going to get colder and recommended that he start feeding some grain along with the big round bales of hay and corn shucks he was feeding. The hay looked to be poor quality and, indeed it was.

Mostly it was grass and weeds cut and baled along the railroad right of way. The corn shucks only served as filler and had very little food value.

A few days later, I was called again see another cow that was down. The cow at least had her head up, but she appeared to be weak and anemic. Her backbone was readily visible as it protruded above the body for about three inches. The abdomen, or barrel, was huge which meant there was a large amount of roughage in the stomachs, but it wasn't moving through. Even though I tried with fluids and vitamins, I knew this cow was going to die. Still, no grain was being fed to the cows.

When I asked the owner again to please feed grain, he replied, "I don't think the cows are starving. I think they are being poisoned on a fungus in the corn stalks." I wondered who put that idea in his head.

I suggested that, if the cow that was now sick died, we send her to the diagnostic laboratory at the University of Illinois for an autopsy. I told him we should also send samples of the large bales of hay, the small bales of hay, and the corn stalks. The hay would need to be tested for its nutritional value and the stalks for fungus.

Within twenty four hours, the cow died and was taken to the diagnostic laboratory.

The owner owned some trucks, so it was easy to transport the cow and roughage samples to the laboratory.

When the veterinary diagnostician phoned me with the results, the first thing he said was "a classic case of starvation." Then he went on to say there was no mold in the corn stalks, the hay from the big bale contained three percent protein while the small square bale was the best with six percent protein. Good hay would have contained at least twelve percent protein. So this really was a starvation ration.

I requested written proof of all the veterinarian told me over the phone because I wanted the owner to see in writing what I had been trying to tell him.

I want to emphasize that these cattle were not deliberately starved. This is merely a case of a person trying to do something that he does not have the knowledge to do.

Sometimes, pride causes a person to do foolish things.

〰〰〰

Nowadays, one can read in the newspaper several times a year about the person or persons who have starved horses, and the confiscating of those horses by humane societies.

My most satisfying case of a starving horse...no, I wasn't satisfied that two young persons I had known all their lives were starving their horse…was the total recovery of a horse that was so weak it could not stand.

I was surprised when Dean Pilson called me to ask me to look at his quarter horse who was down and could not rise. I hadn't seen Dean for quite some time and could hardly believe it when he said they were living where his Dad used to milk cows. I had spent a lot of hours in the barn on that farm treating dairy cows.

When I arrived at the farm, Dean showed me to the milk house where they had moved the horse before he went down. What I found was a recumbent gelding weighing about 850 pounds. The horse's eyes were somewhat dull and so was the hair coat.

"What have you been feeding the horse, Dean?" I asked.

Dean picked up a one pound coffee can and said, "One these filled with oats and a flake of alfalfa hay per day." A flake of hay is about eighteen inches square and four inches thick.

"Not enough, Dean," I said. "He should have been getting a gallon of oats and about three flakes of alfalfa hay per day. An animal needs more feed in cold weather."

"We were feeding what our neighbor recommended."

"Does your neighbor own horses?"

"No."

I said, "I'm going back to my office to get my slings. We need to get this horse up, and the only way to do it is to sling him. Get us a good strong pulley that we can use to lift him."

Had the horse been allowed to lie on the concrete, even with bedding, he would likely have developed decubital ulcers.

I quickly made the fifteen mile round trip to my hospital.

We placed one of the canvas slings in front of the rear legs and one behind the shoulders and connected them with a chain which was attached to a pulley. The pulley was attached to a floor joist which supported the hay mow. By pulling on the rope of the pulley, we lifted the horse to a standing position with his feet just resting on the floor.

Dean got the horse a pail of water, and he readily drank. All the while Dean's wife, Kathy was standing silently by.

I treated the horse intravenously with amino acids and glucose and suggested they offer the horse a small amount of oats. Since there was no manger or feed box where the horse was, I told them they would have to hold the feed and hay while the horse ate.

I took with me to my office a sample of the horse's manure so I could examine it for internal parasite eggs.

When I returned the next day, the horse appeared visibly brighter. He was still drinking water and had eaten a small amout of oats and some hay. I informed them that the fecal exam showed that he had a mild case of stomach worms, but we would wait to worm him when he was feeling better.

After three days, the horse was becoming stronger, so we removed the slings. He was now able to stand on his own and his appetite was improving every day. We dewormed him that day.

As I was carrying my slings out to my truck, I admonished the two smiling young people to keep feeding the horse as I had instructed.

When I went to the Pilson place the next spring to vaccinate the horse with its annual shots, I could see they took me at my word.... the horse was so fat he could hardly walk.

CHAPTER 24

Sam Bergman

Being confronted with many different personalities is the norm for dealing with the public. As I look back on nearly forty years of working with and for people from all walks of life, one person who certainly was different comes to mind.

Sam Bergman was a livestock and grain farmer. He raised corn, soybeans, hay, hogs, and cattle. He possessed a Ph. D. from Purdue University, but I do not know in which discipline. If his degrees were in agriculture, he wasn't putting them to very good use because he was a lousy farmer and raiser of livestock. He was also very eccentric.

He was innovative, however. Instead of a livestock truck to haul his fattened hogs to market, he used an old school bus. Can you imagine the surprised looks on peoples' faces when they passed the bus on the highway, and instead of school children peering out at them, they saw hogs? He did remove the seats so the hogs were standing, not sitting.

Sam's farm bordered that of a dairy farmer named Burt Glendenning. It is an unwritten law (or perhaps it is a written law) that when you stand facing a boundary fence, you are responsible for maintaining the right half of the fence.

Sam's half of the fence became run down with holes in it so that his calves were getting through the fence into Burt's pasture. Burt's half of the fence was well maintained. Sam didn't want to repair the fence, so he suggested to Burt, "Let's trade ends of the fence."

Sam had young children, a son and a daughter. Once when I was dehorning cattle at Sam's farm, the boy asked me how to get the material out of the inside of the horn. Not realizing he intended to do it, I told him to boil the horns in water to soften the material before digging it out of the horn. I should have told him to be sure and boil them outside, because it created a terrible odor.

I didn't, and that probably was a mistake because as I was driving out of the barn lot I saw him heading into the house with a bucket of horns.

I knew about this odor because one time I collected some horns for an assistant scoutmaster and he boiled them on the kitchen stove. A friend of his, who went to his house while he was boiling the horns, said the stench was unbearable.

Sam phoned me once saying he had four cats that he wanted me to "put to sleep." I said, "O.K., Sam, just call for an appointment, or bring them down during our walk-in office hours."

"I can't do that," Sam responded.

"Why not?" I asked.

"They're my wife's cats," he said.

"And she doesn't want to put them to sleep?" I asked.

"I don't know."

"Why don't you ask her?"

"We only talk twice a month in a three way conversation with our psychologist."

"O.K., Call me if you ever get your wife's permission to euthanize her cats."

Needless to say, I didn't euthanize the cats.

CHAPTER **25**

Extra Special Deliveries

It was a cold, miserable day with snow piled up as high as a car along the highways, the wind blowing fifteen miles per hour and the temperature hovering around ten degrees below zero. Needless to say, movement was nearly at a standstill.

I was at a local restaurant with Andy Burke, Fort Dodge pharmaceutical salesman, having a leisurely lunch and then heard, "Dr. Day, you're wanted on the phone," from the waitress.

When I answered the phone, I heard my wife say, "Buck Walters has a ewe that can't have her lambs."

"Okay, call him back and tell him I'll get there as soon as I can," I said.

I thanked Andy for the lunch, said goodbye and was on my way.

It wasn't a fit day for man or beast to be out on the roads, but I had to try to get to the Walters farm.

The first twelve miles were the easy ones. When I came to the gravel road that would take me to my destination, I could see a snowdrift across the road. After turning onto the road, I got out of the car and surveyed the situation. After that initial snowdrift, the road appeared to have only about six inches of snow on it.

I called my wife on the two-way radio and asked her to call Mr. Hendricks, the township road commissioner, and ask him to come out and plow the road to the Walters farm for me. The response I got from my wife was, "His wife said he's asleep, and she won't wake him."

That was Plan A. Now for Plan B. I thought, *"Perhaps if I can blast my way through that drift, I can get all the way to the Walters farm."* Stupid me! I buried the car in the middle of the drift. I couldn't go forward, couldn't back up.

Now for Plan C. This called for me to walk about three-eighths of a mile down the highway in the face of a cold wind in below zero temperatures. Fortunately, I was dressed warmly. Arriving at my destination, I knocked on the door and the farmer, Leonard Cashman, who opened it asked, "Doc, what the heck are you doing out in this kind of weather?"

I had started to explain when he said, "Come on in out of the cold, don't take your boots off, there's a rug in front of the door."

I stepped in, closed the door behind me and then explained my problems to him, asking if he would pull my car out of the snowdrift.

He agreed to help me and then dressed for the occasion.

We rode back down the highway to my car on an Oliver 70 Row Crop tractor with a heat houser. He was driving, and I was standing on the drawbar of the tractor, holding onto the seat.

A heat houser consists of canvas covering the sides of the tractor engine and directing the heat of the engine backwards toward the driver. The canvases, along with a plastic windshield, are supposed to keep the driver warm.

Arriving back at my car, Leonard backed the tractor up to my car, and I attached one end of a log chain to the drawbar of the tractor and the other end to the hitch on my car. Slowly, he edged the tractor forward and backed the car out of the drift.

As I unhooked the chain from the tractor, he leaned down from the seat so I could hear him and said, "Stop at the house. I'll go with you, and we'll go along the river and maybe there will be less snow."

We drove west about a half mile and then turned right on the road paralleling the river. Leonard was right...there was less snow on this road because the trees lining the banks of the river kept the snow from blowing on the road.

Good progress was made until we got about two hundred yards from the road that would take us into the Walters' barnyard. Another snowdrift blocked our way. I said, "It looks like we walk from here."

I took all the equipment I thought I would need and some I didn't think I would need because I didn't want to be walking back and forth from car to barn. Fortunately, Leonard was there to help me pack the stuff.

The Walters family was watching for us, so when we walked into the barnyard aglow with light from a pole lamp, father and son came out of the house.

"Where's the ewe?" I asked.

"In the brooder house," was the reply.

The brooder house was just that. It was designed to get baby chicks started on their way to adulthood. The house was probably ten by twelve feet in area, but the roof was the interesting part of it. It was actually one fourth of a circle. The top of the roof was about seven feet high at the front of the building and curved to the ground at the back.

My parents had a brooder house just like this one where we started one or two hundred baby chicks each spring. Ground corncobs were used to cover the floor of the house for the baby chicks. The brooder stood in the center of the house. As I recall the brooder stood on adjustable legs so that it could be raised as the chicks grew. Through the use of light bulbs and a reflector, the brooder provided warmth for the chicks. Small troughs held the chicks' feed, and water was supplied in jars turned upside down. Actually, the brooder appeared to look like my vision of a UFO.

The ewe was in a pen in the middle of the brooder house, and it was sort of crowded when the four of us entered. I climbed over the two feet high fence with a bucket of warm water, some lubricant and an obstetrical sleeve. It was a job to get my right arm out of my coveralls and sweatshirt before rolling up my shirt sleeve and donning my plastic o. b. sleeve. Examination of the ewe revealed a pelvis too small for the lamb to pass through, so I prepared to do a Caesarean section.

After clipping the small amount of wool from the ewe's abdomen, I proceeded to cleanse and disinfect the skin. The wool of a sheep is very oily.

Remember, the temperature outside the brooder house was minus ten degrees Fahrenheit. The temperature inside wasn't much higher... the only heat we had was provided by a one hundred watt heat lamp inside an aluminum reflector. Of course, we did have some hot air floating around from the talking of the four of us men in the house.

After draping the abdomen of the ewe, I picked up my scalpel and started to incise the skin of the abdomen. About that time the Walters' son, Denny, said, "Doc, I think I'm going to faint." Since he was on his knees at the head of the ewe, I said, "Go ahead, just don't fall over on the ewe."

He hung the upper part of his body over the low fence surrounding the pen so he did not interfere with my surgery. His head nearly touched the straw covered floor.

Now that I knew Denny's falling would not impede my surgery, I continued my incision through the skin, muscle and peritoneum, the inner layer of the abdomen. Grasping the body of the uterus, I lifted it to the outside and incised it before removing a large lamb from one of the horns. Handing the lamb to Buck Walters to dry with a towel, I began to move the other lamb out of the horn and through the incision in the uterus. When I had the lamb out, I handed it to Denny, who had recovered by now, to dry off with the towel.

When I placed one of my warm stainless steel instruments down in the cold, stainless steel pan, it immediately froze to the bottom.

After inserting an antibiotic bolus in each horn of the uterus, I began to place sutures in the uterine incision.

And that was when I got my first whiff of smoke. I looked up toward the roof and saw smoke coming from the cord that supplied electricity to the heat lamp. Buck immediately unplugged the cord and threw the lamp outside. Not only was my source of heat gone, but the small light bulb in the dome of the building didn't supply enough light to allow me to see where to place the sutures. After the heat lamp was replaced by a trouble lamp, I had enough illumination to complete the surgery.

Leonard and I lugged my equipment back to my car and headed home. Before we got to Leonard's farm, I said, "You know, Leonard, it takes a darn fool to do something like that in weather like this." He responded with, "Doc, I was thinking the same thing all the time you were operating on that ewe."

Leonard quit farming and moved away shortly after that, and I rarely see him. When I do, however, he always relates to me how many times he has told the story about that night delivering lambs by C-section.

❧❧❧

I had made seventeen farm visits and probably driven two hundred miles to treat sick livestock that day, and I was bone tired. But I still had a Caesarean section to perform on a sow after I had eaten my dinner.

When I walked into the kitchen, I noticed that my wife, Mary Jane, was wearing a pair of my work coveralls while she served dinner to our three children.

"What's going on, why are you wearing a pair of my coveralls?" I asked.

"I'm going with you to do that surgery," she answered.

"What about the kids?"

"I have a baby sitter lined up; I'm going to get her while you're eating."

As soon as she had placed my plate on the table she was out the door.

By the time Mary Jane and the baby sitter returned, I had finished eating and was ready to leave on the farm visit.

We drove the eight or ten miles to the farm where the sow awaited me. I had seen her earlier in the day and had given her an injection of oxytocin to see if I could get her uterus to contract and expel the pigs to no avail.

On the way to the farm, I wondered how my wife would react to working on her knees in the straw with which the floor of the sow pen was bedded. She was excellent help for me when doing small animal surgeries, but had not yet been out with me to do surgery on the farm. She was very willing to help me, however.

The farmer was waiting outside the barn in his pickup truck when we arrived. The sow was also waiting for us, only she was lying peacefully on her side. She was breathing easily and, other than an occasional slight straining with fluid being expelled from the vulva, one would not know she was in labor.

I gave the sow an injection of tranquilizer and, while waiting for it to take effect, I started to get out my instruments and arrange them in the stainless steel pan. I then clipped the area on her left side where I would make the incision through the skin and muscles so I could reach the uterus. After cleansing the area well, I ran a line block of anesthetic where I would make my incision.

With all else ready, I placed a sterile drape over the surgical area and made my incision through the body wall. I immediately found the neck of the uterus and made my incision in front of the cervix.

When I pulled the first pig out of the sow, the farmer let out a little groan and fell to his side in a dead faint. I handed the pig to my wife who was waiting with a towel to dry it. By the time she had the first pig dried and placed under the heat lamp, I had another one ready for her. Along about the third pig, the farmer recovered enough to sit up, but showed no interest in helping with the pigs. All in all, we delivered eight very large pigs, too large for a first time porcine mother.

Once again, I was thankful for my wife for if I had relied on the farmer to help, the pigs and I would have been in trouble.

Not all the Caesarean sections that I did were on sheep, swine and cattle. I have also done several on dogs and cats, and even chinchillas. I once did a C-section on a goat assisted by a surgical nurse from a nearby hospital.

I was called to tend a nanny goat that was in labor. It was a cold night and the goat was in a pen with a dirt floor…no straw for bedding.

Catching the goat, I asked the lady owner to hold her head while I examined her. When I inserted my plastic covered hand into the goat's vagina, I could feel a big nose, a really big nose. I also discovered that the nanny had been trying for more than a little while. There was no lubrication…this would be a dry birth, if I could even deliver the kid.

I attempted to deliver the kid, but to no avail.

It was then I informed the owner that we would need to remove the baby goat by Caesarean section. I also told her that I would like to do it in the warmth of my animal hospital, rather than in the stall where we were then.

She said, "I'll have to phone my sister. She's singing with a group up at Beaverville. She's a surgical nurse at Central Hospital."

I told her that I would head back to my office and get ready for the surgery.

About forty-five minutes later, they arrived with the goat in the back of a pickup truck. It was no problem to bring the goat into the surgery room where I first gave it an injection of tranquilizer.

The goat was very tractable when we lifted her onto the surgery table, rolled her over onto her back, and hydraulically raised her to working height. After clipping the small amount of hair on her, I scrubbed, disinfected and draped her abdomen. I then ran a line block of local anesthetic and was ready for surgery.

When I opened my sterile pack of instruments, the nurse among us said, "You use the same instruments we do where I work."

I replied, "Yes, only I own my own instruments. The hospital provides those the doctors use."

When I started surgery she said, "You do it just like we do at the hospital."

I cut into the goat and brought the uterine horn containing the kid outside the abdomen. When I removed the fetus, I knew the goat had been in labor for some time. There was no placenta. She had passed it while trying to give birth. The baby was very large.

Closure of the uterus, abdominal wall and skin were routine. An injection of antibiotics and oxytocin to shrink the uterus were given, and the goat was ready to return home.

2222

One Saturday morning I received a phone call from Rick Munster informing me that he had a beef cow "that couldn't have her calf." Rick was a slow talking bachelor that lived about sixteen miles north of where my hospital was situated. Rick sometimes fed his cows too well and I assumed the cow's problem was that she was too fat and the calf couldn't get through the birth canal. Okay, a little assistance with the fetal extractor and the calf should come right out.

I drove to Rick's farm and, after examining the cow, determined that in addition to the cow being too fat, the calf was too large. Unfortunately, I didn't have my sterile instrument pack with me. So, it was back to my office to get the instruments to do the job.

When I returned to Rick's farm, I couldn't believe my eyes. There were cars and pickup trucks parked everywhere. Then I walked into the barn -- there more people than there were vehicles parked outside.

"What's going on?" I asked Rick.

"Oh, I just asked a few of the neighbors over to watch you do surgery. This doesn't happen very often around here." I thought about asking him if he had charged admission. "Perhaps that was how he was going to pay me for my services," I thought to myself.

The surgery went well and I delivered a large, healthy bull calf. I'm sure my reputation as a large animal surgeon was enhanced as a result of performing in front of that audience..

2222

The only time I had a larger audience was at the University of

Illinois when I was asked to demonstrate a Caesarean section on a female swine at a conference for veterinarians.

Mary Jane went with me so that she could visit her parents while I was at the meeting.

I had made a couple of farm calls early in the morning and one took longer than I had anticipated, so we were running late.

About half way between our home and Urbana, we were pulled over for speeding by an Illinois State Trooper. As I pulled over to the side of the road, he pulled in behind me and motioned me back to his car. As I approached the police car, I could see that the trooper was "Hooley" Marlette. His beagle dog was a patient of mine.

As I approached the car, "Hooley" said, "I'm not going to give you a ticket, I just want to ask you some questions about my dog."

I told him I was on my way to a conference at the University of Illinois and was running late so, after he had asked the questions and I had answered them, we were on our way again.

After Mary Jane dropped me off at the Large Animal Clinic, I sought out Dr. George Wood. He was the person who had asked me to do the surgery demonstration and who was responsible for acquiring the pregnant sow.

When I found him, I asked to see the patient. We walked down through the LAC to the pen holding the hog. It was young gilt…a female hog that has never given birth to pigs. I have to say I was a little disappointed.

I looked at the pig…she wasn't old enough or big enough to be called a hog.

As I looked over the fence at the little female, I said, "Dr. Wood, she's not pregnant."

He looked at me and smiled and replied, "She's just a little pregnant."

I smiled back at him and said, "There's no such thing as being a little bit pregnant. She either is or she isn't."

The surgery went well and although there were no baby pigs to show the audience, I at least was able to teach them the technique.

CHAPTER **26**

Horsin' Around

As a student interning with Dr. Strahler at Abingdon, Illinois, I was exposed to my first serious horse injury in the field. I had seen horses in the large animal clinic at the U of I that were being treated for injuries sustained elsewhere, but the initial treatment had been performed prior to the horse's arrival at the clinic.

We were called to treat a horse with a badly lacerated right rear leg, but did not know until we arrived that the injured animal was an unbroken two year-old quarter horse. The colt had never even seen a halter, much less worn one.

When we arrived the colt was in a fairly large corral, and the only way to handle him was to rope and tie him to one of the corral posts. Dr. Strahler was good with a rope and he snagged him at once. We tied the colt to a post and immediately placed a halter on him. For an unbroken horse, he didn't resist too much.

Dr. Strahler put a twitch on the horse's upper lip and twisted the handle and then gave the handle to me hold, along with the halter rope, while he injected the anesthetic into the horse's jugular vein. Soon the horse went down on his side, but Dr. Strahler continued to administer anesthetic until the horse was under deep enough for surgery to be performed. It was then we could tell the horse had lacerated the skin and tendon of his right rear leg.

After cleansing the wound, an "x" suture was placed between the severed ends of the tendon, before suturing the skin. Cotton and gauze were wrapped around the leg and then a plaster of paris cast was applied. About this time, the horse was beginning to wake up, but was kept down until we knew he would be steady enough on his feet to walk to the stall in the barn.

It was unfortunate but we didn't have a hydraulic table (or even an operating room), nor a horse gurney nor recovery room. The bare ground of the horse lot served as the surgery table, the horse's feet served as the gurney, and the horse stall was the recovery room.

Dr. Strahler and his family left the following morning to visit his parents in Ohio. At one p.m., the owners of the horse phoned to say that the horse had broken the plaster cast down.

It was less than a half mile to the barn where the horse was stalled, and I arrived there in no time at all. As the owner and I were walking to the barn I asked, "Can you get a lead rope attached to the halter?"

His reply was, "Not me, I'm not getting in the stall with that horse."

So I opened the door and managed to grab the horse's halter. I was surprised when the horse didn't pull back and resist, so I quickly snapped the lead rope on to the halter. Handing the rope through the space between the bars of the stall to the owner, I then closed the door. After placing the twitch on the horse's upper lip, I placed the handle in the right hand of the owner, admonishing him to keep a tight hold on it.

Shrugging my shoulders, moving my arms, and taking deep breaths, I screwed up enough courage to open the door and approach the right hind leg of the horse. The owner was doing a good job with the twitch, so I moved my hand down the leg toward the hoof. Thankfully, the horse didn't seem to be frightened and didn't move a muscle. When a horse is upset, they will usually lay back their ears, but his were still upright.

Still wary that the horse might kick me, I took a pair of tin snips out of my rear pocket and started to cut away the broken down cast. Ordinary scissors were not strong enough to cut through the plaster of paris. Amazingly, the horse never moved. It was if he had been handled many times and was used to someone rubbing a hand down his leg. Finally, I had successfully removed the cast. Next would come the taped bandages under the cast. I removed the bandages and examined the wound. Thankfully, all the sutures were still in place.

Now I had a decision to make. Should I attempt to recast the leg, or should I just put a nice strong bandage on the leg and cover it with a track bandage like the ones used on race horses?

Realizing that we couldn't stand there holding the horse long enough for the plaster of paris to dry sufficiently, I opted for the bandage.

With the rebandaging completed, I exited the stall and removed the twitch from the horse's upper lip. Then I could reach through the bars of the stall and unsnap the lead rope from the halter.

I almost had to kick myself to make sure it had not been a dream about removing the cast and applying a new bandage.

Reminding the owner I would return the next day to apply a new bandage, I left for more farm calls.

I returned to the horse barn the following day and changed the bandage just as easily as I had previously and the procedure went off without a hitch. Perhaps Dr. Strahler should add an additional charge for breaking the horse to the halter and lead rope.

We had to leave to return to school before the Strahler family returned, so I left him a message about the horse, reminding him he should see it the following day.

My older brother, who farmed near the town, kept me abreast of the horse's progress and boosted my ego a little when he told me what a great job the owner thought I did in treating the horse.

༻༻༻༺

It was another one of those two a.m. calls when I drove about twelve miles north of Watseka to see a horse allegedly hit by a car.

I don't know how fast the convertible was going when it hit the horse that was moseying across the highway, but it was going fast enough to throw the horse over the windshield, over the front seat, and into the back seat of the car.

It was hard to believe that a one thousand pound horse could be lifted high enough in the air to clear the hood, windshield and front seat to land on its back in the back seat. All four legs of the dead horse were pointing toward the sky.

And the driver and his passenger...they were fine.

❧❧❧

On another occasion, I was called to again see a horse that had been struck by a car. This was at Iroquois, a small town northeast of Watseka.

In order to get there in a hurry, because I didn't know if the horse was dead or alive, I took the blacktopped country roads.

When I arrived, I could see the horse was dead. The driver and her passenger were standing there talking with the apparent driver puffing away on a cigarette.

Soon, we could hear the siren of the approaching ambulance. It came into sight as it crossed the bridge over the Iroquois River.

As soon as the cigarette puffing lady saw the ambulance, she threw the cigarette to the ground and grabbed the back of her neck while saying, "Oh! Oh!"

I knew the owner of the horse, and I thought to myself, *"I hope you're not thinking about an insurance settlement from the horse owner, because it's highly doubtful he has any insurance, and he certainly doesn't have any money."*

❧❧❧

One of my favorite horse patients was a retired Standardbred racehorse stallion named Sharon's Rose.

In retirement for many years and now nearly thirty years old, the horse spent his days grazing in the confines of a three acre pasture surrounded by a white board fence.

In addition to the attractive fence around the pasture, the owner kept the pasture neatly mowed so there were no unsightly weeds and provided a nice building to protect the horse from the weather.

Did I mention that the pasture was along a heavily trafficked highway?

Sharon's Rose was living the Life of Riley until.....one day a truck hauling garbage from Chicago to a dump farther south lost one of its outside dual wheels on the left side of the trailer. It also lost its outside wheel on the right side of the trailer.

The right wheel rolled into a soybean field on the west side of the highway.

The left wheel crashed through the fence on the north side of the pasture and rolled toward Sharon's Rose.

Hearing the crash as the wheel smashed through the fence, the horse, with his tail toward the fence, lifted his head from grazing and turned his head toward the sound of the crash.

The moving wheel struck the horse's shoulder a glancing blow and barely grazed the skin above the eye and rolled for a few more feet.

I was called to treat the horse who was not badly injured...just a small cut above the eye and an abrasion on the shoulder...requiring only a tetanus antitoxin injection and a tube of ointment to be applied to the cut.

I ask you, what are the odds of a rolling wheel striking a horse in the middle of a three acre pasture?

♪♪♪♪

Each time I passed Dick Moss' farm when I was on a call, I would see the old white pony in the small pasture west of the house. The pony had belonged to Dick's children who were all married and away from the farm.

The pony was fat, and its coat was slick. One could only tell that it was lame if it moved. The lower joint of the right front leg was bent due to ankylosis...a stiffness of the joint due to abnormal adhesion and rigidity of the bones. In this case, the pony walked on the outside of the foot.

Dick engaged the services of a farrier to trim the hoof each month. The pony was not in any pain from the condition.

It was a rainy morning when Dick, with some of the words catching in his throat, phoned and asked me to come out and "put the pony to sleep."

When I asked him why he had decided to euthanize old "Buck", he replied that a person from an SPCA chapter a few miles north was driving down the road and saw the pony hobbling across the pasture the previous day.

The person stopped and rang Dick's doorbell. According to Dick the person was very blunt when he said, "Either get that pony's leg fixed, or put him to sleep." Being a very mild mannered person, Dick offered no argument or defense, just said, "Yes, sir."

Knowing how much the nineteen year-old pony meant to Dick and his family, I told him that I would go to bat for him and explain to the SPCA the reason for the lameness and that nothing could be done. I would also explain to them that Dick was doing all he could for the pony, and that the pony was in very little pain.

Dick said, "No, Doc, I don't want to be a troublemaker, just come up and put him to sleep."

It was raining fairly hard when I got out of my car at the Moss farm. I filled a large syringe with euthanasia solution and knocked on the back door of the house. A sad looking Dick opened the door. "He's in the pasture, Doc. I don't want to see you do it."

By the time I reached the pony, it was pouring down rain. I attached a lead rope to the halter ring and wished Dick was there to hold onto the lead rope. I had a problem. I had no one to hold the horse's head still when I inserted the needle into the jugular vein.

Removing the needle from the big plastic syringe, I placed the syringe in the chest pocket of my coveralls. Using the thumb of my left hand, I shut off the flow of blood and quickly jabbed the needle into the vein. Seeing blood oozing from the needle, I grabbed the syringe from my pocket and connected it to the syringe.

I quickly injected the solution into the vein, removed the needle and jumped back, lest the pony fall on me. Fortunately, he first dropped to his knees and then rolled over on his side. I waited until I was sure the heart had stopped beating before I removed the lead rope and walked back to my car.

I didn't stop at the house to be paid. I knew Dick would either phone me to ask the amount he owed me, or wait until I sent a statement at the end of the month.

The following day, I received a call from the SPCA member asking if I had been to see the pony owned by Dick Moss.

When I replied in the affirmative, he asked what I had done.

I replied that since there was no treatment that would cure the pony, I had "put him to sleep."

He said, "You didn't have to do that."

"That's not what Dick Moss understood," I replied and went on to tell him, "When I am old and feeble and lame, I hope someone like you doesn't come around and tell my children to put me to sleep."

♪♪♪

Although this story has nothing to do with my veterinary practice, it is an indication of why I became a veterinarian.

When I was ten years-old I went home after delivering my paper route one afternoon, and in front of the barn there stood a black and white Shetland pony. Never mind that he had spent most of his life pulling coal carts from deep in the mine to the surface. Never mind that he was considerably older than I. To me, he was the most beautiful pony I had ever seen.

Not long after that, my dad brought home a pony buggy which we soon converted into a wagon. He removed the body of the buggy from the running gear and constructed a wagon box, which he then placed on the running gear. After adding a seat to the wagon box, I became an entrepreneur.

I already had a paper route, delivering 86 newspapers six days a week. I was fattening a small pig that I had purchased with a five dollar birthday gift. In four months , I would sell the pig for slaughter.

Now I could collect newspapers, rags and metal to sell to the local junkyard. This was during World War II and those items were in great demand.

The money I made from these enterprises would be used to purchase savings stamps and, eventually, War Bonds. This was after I bought a new baseball glove and bicycle, though.

After my Shetland pony, I owned a larger white pony and then a three-gaited saddle mare.

Once I started high school, I lost all interest in horses and concentrated on sports and raising pigs for 4-H and FFA.

CHAPTER 27

Shocking Events

My first experience with death by lightning strike came when I was an intern with Dr. Bob Strahler at Abingdon, Illinois, during the summer between my third and fourth years of veterinary school.

After a particularly nasty rainstorm with much thunder and lightning, we were called to see the results of a lightning strike on a tree where cattle had congregated to get out of the rain.

What we found were eleven Angus cows and an Angus bull, all killed when lightning struck the tree.

Although it was obvious from the scar that extended from high up on the tree down the trunk to the ground, the animals still had to be examined by a veterinarian so the farmer could collect from the insurance company for the loss of the animals.

$$\text{رررر}$$

Shortly after graduation from veterinary school, I was called to examine another cow that had allegedly been struck by lightning.

Instead of being in a group of cattle, this cow was lying alone in a small ditch at the bottom of a hill. It was July in Illinois, the weather had been hot, and the cow had been dead for three or four days..... the essentials for an animal to begin putrefaction. A positive diagnosis of death by lightning strike is difficult at best, but is made much more difficult when dealing with an animal that has been dead for several days.

As I wended my way down the hill toward the cow, I was reviewing in my mind the clues I had been taught to look for in the case of an animal suspected of being killed by lightning. When I reached the animal, I knew that all I had been taught about death by lightning stroke would be of no avail due to the advanced deterioration of the cow.

I knelt down by the cow in preparation for slicing into the foreleg to look for injection of the blood vessels of the tendons, a supposedly telltale sign of death by lightning and immediately decided if I were to continue my career as a veterinarian, I would need to have a really strong stomach in order to stand the smell of dead animals.

The cut ends of the tendon revealed very little that would help me make a positive diagnosis of death by lightning due to advanced putrefaction. However, a question by the owner, who was standing above me on the hill, aided immensely in the diagnosis. As I looked up to the man to answer his question, I noticed that the leaves were wilted on the south side of three trees growing in a line coming down the hillside. This was an indication that the streak of lightning had come down the hill and struck and killed the cow.

On a sheet of our practice letterhead paper, I wrote that I had determined the cow had been killed by lightning, signed it and gave it to the owner to present to his insurance company.

About two days later, the farmer appeared at the veterinary office and said, "Doc, the insurance company isn't going to pay me for the cow. The agent came out to the farm, stood at the top of the hill, looked down at the cow and said she wasn't killed by lightning."

This really got my dander up. Who was this insurance agent? He was not a veterinarian, nor was he a farmer. Yet, he had the audacity to say that my diagnosis was wrong. This could not happen. After all, I was a recent graduate of the University of Illinois College of Veterinary Medicine. I had passed all my courses and the examination administered by the State of Illinois Office of Professional Regulation to become a licensed veterinarian. How dare this insurance agent question my abilities? As I look back on this case, I realize I might have been a little proud of being a newly licensed veterinarian and I was hurt by the fact that someone had questioned my abilities.

I sat down and wrote the insurance company another letter in which I explained in detail why, in my opinion, the cow had been killed by lightning strike. I must confess that the fact that I was irate over the agent's questioning of my diagnosis probably showed through in the letter.

At any rate, it turned out well as the insurance company paid the farmer for his loss of the cow.

〜〜〜

I believe the only other multiple loss of animal life I have seen came when three horses were struck in an open pasture. The horses were all in a line facing south, and the lightning came down through two large catalpa trees and struck all three horses simultaneously.

〜〜〜

Seldom does lightning strike a single animal in the middle of a treeless field. The one case I saw of this happening is still vivid in my mind. A two thousand pound Belgian stallion, wearing metal shoes, was hit apparently in the shoulder by lightning… or the lightning hit the ground and was attracted to the metal shoe.

In any case, the horse dropped dead in its tracks, its leg split wide open from the hoof to the shoulder.

〜〜〜

Not every animal death that the owner suspected of being caused by lightning was caused by lightning. Occasionally, an owner would find an animal dead in the pasture after a rainstorm and think immediately -- killed by lightning. Or perhaps, the owner would try to collect insurance on an animal that he knew died from other causes.

Once I was called to see a dead four hundred pound calf that was allegedly struck by lightning in the middle of a small pasture. The first thing I noticed when I looked at the calf was that he was very thin, almost to the point of dehydration. Then I noticed the string of yellow mucus hanging from one nostril and the yellow matter in the eyes.

At that point, I asked the owner if the calf was the offspring of one of the cows I saw in the pasture. He replied that no, he had just purchased the calf at a sales barn the previous week.

I explained to the owner that the calf appeared to have "shipping fever", a term applied to cattle that had been moved through sales barns where they picked up viruses and bacteria that caused respiratory diseases. Often, two or three different viruses and bacteria could be isolated from the calves so affected.

I explained that I could do an autopsy on the dead calf to confirm my diagnosis, but the owner declined.

❧❧❧❧

A dairy farmer once called me to look at a cow that he thought had been killed by lightning. As in other cases where the farmer suspected death of an animal by lightning, it had rained the night before.

Arriving at the farm, I inquired of the farmer of the location of the cow. He replied, "She's in the barn."

I thought to myself, "This would be a first, a cow hit by lightning in the barn and the barn didn't even catch on fire."

All the Holstein cows were lined up in a row of stanchions, peacefully chewing their cuds. The owner had finished the morning milking about an hour before I arrived.

"She's the third from the end, Doc," said the owner.

"How do you think she was hit by lightning, and the two cows between her and the wall of the barn weren't hit?" I asked.

"The barn door was open, and I figure it came through the door and hit and killed her," replied the farmer.

After a discussion between the two of us, I finally convinced the man that lightning is not that selective -- that it can't bend around two cows to reach a third, that if the cow in question had been killed by lightning, and then the other two would also have been hit.

ᴊᴊᴊ

I believe that my best example of a farmer who has lost livestock trying to collect unearned insurance is the time I was called to examine three dead cows allegedly killed by lightning. True, the cows were in a pasture with several trees. True, the cows were lying dead about fifty feet apart. Also true, we hadn't had rain in more than ten days.

"I don't believe your cows were killed by lightning, because we haven't had a rain in the last ten days," I told the farmer.

"My neighbor, Joe, had a cow hit by lightning."

"When?" I asked.

"About two weeks ago."

I rest my case.

I walked up to the nearest cow, placed my fist into the area of her flank, and pushed down very hard. It felt like trying to push on hardened concrete.

"What have you been feeding these cows?" I asked.

"Fines," he replied.

The word "fines" is applied to the screenings from corn that is being elevated up into storage bins. The tips of the corn kernels break off and flutter to the ground. It is okay to sweep them up and combine them with other grain to feed the animals, but if the animal eats too many of the "fines" with little or no roughage, the rumen stops working. Then, when the animal drinks a lot of water, it's like adding water to a bag of concrete mix.

"The problem with these cows is that they overate on 'fines' and then drank a lot of water. They were unable to move the grain through their digestive tract, and they foundered. They essentially died of toxic indigestion," I told the farmer.

"Then, you aren't going to tell my insurance company they were killed by lightning?"

"No sir," I replied.

I was never called to see an animal on that farm again.

❧❧❧

At times, animals are affected by a short in an electrical system, just as if they had been hit by lightning.

A friend of mine, who is also a veterinarian, was called by one of his clients who fed beef cattle for market. The farmer complained that he had three fat steers that dropped dead while they were walking across the feedlot.

My friend drove out to the farm, and while he was standing by the fence observing the cattle another steer fell dead.

It turned out that there was a bare electrical wire buried in the muddy feedlot, and when an animal came near the wire it died from electrocution.

❧❧❧

One of my best large animal clients phoned me once to tell me he needed me to come out to his farm to see a five hundred pound heifer that couldn't get to her feet. He said, "Doc, she tries, but can only rise about half way to her feet and then falls back down."

When I arrived at the farm, I found the heifer lying in front of the water tank. The float on the tank had apparently malfunctioned, and water had spilled over the tank's wall and soaked the bedding in front of the tank. This is where the heifer was lying.

As I was observing the heifer, I noticed the floating heater in the water tank. Since it was winter, the heater was necessary to keep the water in the tank from freezing.

Presently, the heifer attempted to rise, but only got half way before she fell back to the normal position.

"Let's unplug the water heater," I said.

As soon as the water heater was unplugged, the heifer arose and walked away.

Apparently the float in the tank wasn't the only piece of equipment that wasn't working properly. There was a short in the heater which was electrifying the water, the tank and the wet ground around the tank. The shock wasn't enough to kill the animal, but did keep her from rising.

⟡⟡⟡⟡

Another farmer with an electrical short in a water heater wasn't quite so lucky. When he went out to his feedlot to check his cattle one morning, he found three steers dead at the water fountain.

He was puzzled about the deaths, because the day before all steers were at the trough eating and appeared healthy to him. This is the information he gave me when he phoned me to come out to his farm.

As we walked to the three dead steers, I glanced around at the other cattle and could see none that appeared sickly.

Two of the dead steers were lying away from the automatic watering device, but the third had fallen with its head against the metal base of the water fountain. This was fortunate for it created a ground and kept the other cattle from being electrocuted.

I recommended to the farmer that he cut off the electricity to the water fountain and call an electrician to repair it.

CHAPTER 28

Palomino Dog

Over the years, I treated many animals and some of those animals left a more lasting impression on me than others. One such animal was Palomino dog, commonly known as Pal, a blonde mixed Cocker Spaniel, hence the name. I believe the other half of her heritage was Dachshund.

Since she had strayed to one of the Standardbred horse farms where I performed the veterinary services, she had followed me around when I was out there treating the animals.

Periodically, I vaccinated all the horses on the farm. Since there were always a number of horses to be vaccinated, I would place my supply of vaccines, disposable syringes, cotton balls and alcohol in a wheelbarrow to transport them through the barns.

Invariably, Pal would sit and look longingly up at the wheelbarrow, so I would pick her up and place her in the space not occupied by my supplies. As I pushed the wheelbarrow from stall to stall, Pal would enjoy her free ride.

On one of my visits to treat a sick horse the owner, Joe Roberts, asked if I would take a look at the yearlings in the pasture up on the hill as he suspected one or more might be ill. Since I felt I might need some medicines to treat the sick ones, I decided to drive my pickup to the pasture. As I approached my truck, I saw Pal sitting by the driver's side door. I reached down, picked her up and placed her in the bed of my pickup.

There were about seven or eight yearlings in the group at the hill pasture. I immediately saw the colt that Joe was concerned about. I said, "Joe, he's really sick, let's get him down to the barn."

I drove my truck back to the barn and Joe led the colt. Because I was thinking about the sick colt, I forgot that Pal was riding in the bed of my pickup.

Upon examining the yearling colt, I found he was suffering from pneumonia and had a temperature of 106 degrees. I treated the colt with antibiotics and told Joe that I would return in the afternoon to check on him again.

I drove back to my office to get some supplies that I would need on my next farm visit, picked up my supplies and returned to my truck. To my surprise, there was Pal standing on her rear legs with her forelegs on top of the side of the pickup bed wagging her tail.

Thankful that she hadn't jumped out of the truck while I was driving down the road, I carried her into the hospital and placed her in a holding cage that was used for dogs in for grooming. I also provided her with drinking water.

After lunch, I returned to the animal hospital, carried Pal out to the truck, placed her in the cab with me and headed for the horse farm to check on the colt I had treated earlier.

When Joe saw me lift Pal out of my truck and place her on the ground, he laughingly asked, "Were you trying to steal my dog?"

Upon examining the colt, I found him to be much improved and made arrangements to return the following morning to treat him again.

When I walked through the door of the barn, I saw Pal standing by the door of the truck and wagging her tail as if to say, "I want to go for another ride."

Each year when it was time Pal's yearly vaccinations and heartworm exam, I would say to her, "C'mon, Pal, it's time for your shots," she would walk over to me and sit at my feet. I would kneel, administer the two shots and draw a blood sample from her foreleg and she would never move.

When I removed the sutures from her spay incision, she just lay on her back in front of the horse barn and didn't move as I snipped her sutures.

CHAPTER 29

Poisoned Pets

In my experience, most cases of poisoning in pets is accidental, however, occasionally a neighbor reacts to a perceived wrong brought on by the pet of someone in the neighborhood. Generally, in an intentional poisoning case, the perpetrator feels wronged by a neighbor who allows his pet to defecate in his yard or urinate on his shrubbery. Sometimes the perceived wrong is caused by a neighbor's cat urinating in a flower bed and digging up the flowers while attempting to bury the waste.

Both the owner and the animal are harmed by a neighbor who poisons a pet out of spite. The animal suffers injury or death. The owner suffers financially and mentally. He is burdened financially by an unexpected veterinary bill and mentally from the thought that a neighbor willfully harmed his pet.

The only case that I felt was intentional poisoning occurred to a dog owned by Sandy, also the owner of the snake mentioned in another chapter.

Sandy brought her dog, Lady, to my hospital one afternoon because she was experiencing convulsions. From the other signs exhibited by Lady, I suspected aldrin poisoning. Aldrin was one of the chlorinated hydrocarbon insecticides banned from being sold in the 1970's.

The only way I knew to treat Lady was to control the convulsions until the effects of the poison wore off. So I immediately injected Lady intravenously with sodium pentobarbital until she stopped convulsing and was breathing normally. Then I taped the syringe in place so I could administer more anesthetic as needed.

We kept Lady in our hospital for observation until closing time. Since no one would be at the hospital during the night, we asked Sandy to pick her up before we closed the office. The agreement with Sandy was that she could call me any time during the night if she felt that I was needed.

Unfortunately, I was needed at two a. m. because Lady was convulsing again. With Lady lying on the kitchen table, I again gave her enough anesthetic to control the convulsions. Fortunately, that treatment was the last Lady needed, because the next morning Sandy brought her to the hospital for me to remove the needle from her front leg vein.

ᒋᒋᒋᒐ

It was not long after I opened my practice that an excited man came rushing into my office with his limp dog in his arms. As he laid the dog on the table, I could see it was not breathing. I checked for a heartbeat, but there was none.

"I'm sorry, sir, she's dead." I told him.

"But she was alive fifteen minutes ago."

I queried him as to what led up to the dog's dying.

"We are poisoning pigeons at the church where I am the minister. I saw a pigeon fall from the sky, and my dog ran over and bit into the bird. Within a minute, the dog started convulsing. She only stopped when I pulled up in front of your office."

"What are you using to poison the pigeons?" I asked.

"It's a strychnine compound," he answered and handed me the instructions.

I read the instructions, and then did some quick calculations.

"I think you should remove the strychnine compound from the

belfry," I said. "This is so strong that if a child touched the feet of a dead pigeon and then stuck his finger in his mouth, he would die."

That was my first case of strychnine poisoning in the dog, but not my last.

꘎꘎꘎

A lady I didn't know walked into my office one morning accompanied by a dog with blood dripping from its ear tip. As she walked up to the counter in the waiting room, she said, "I called my vet, and he told me to bring my dog into his office tomorrow. I didn't want to wait that long, though."

As I entered her and her dog's information into the computer, I learned that she lived about twenty miles from my hospital, and her usual veterinarian lived another twelve miles beyond that.

Once the dog was on the examining table, I could see the dripping blood was very thin, so I suspected Warfarin poisoning from rat or mouse bait.

I asked her if she lived in the country or in town and she replied, "in the country." I then asked if her husband was a farmer and she replied, "No, we just rent the house on this farm."

"Do you have any rat poison out around the barn?"

"No, we don't rent the barn...the farmer may have some poison out though. Oh, I saw our dog walking across the barn lot with a rat in its mouth yesterday."

I surmised the dog had eaten the dead rat thus exposing him to the effects of the anti-clotting agent in the rat bait. Then he probably tried to catch a rat and was bitten on the ear, and that was the source of the bleeding. Normally a small bite on the ear would have started to heal by now, but the thinned blood would not clot.

I informed the lady that I would need to keep the dog to treat it with Vitamin K1. Sometimes, I could inject the drug into the muscle, but I had decided that, in this dog's condition, I should inject the KI intravenously. In order to do that, I would mix the proper dosage of Vitamin K1 in a 250 milliliter bottle of sterile saline and let it drip slowly into the dog's vein. Undiluted Vitamin K1 injected directly into the vein could kill the dog.

The following morning the dog was feeling much better, so when the lady phoned I told her it could go home.

When she came, I dispensed some Vitamin K1 tablets for her to give the dog for several days.

Since I never heard from this client again, I assume the dog recovered from the poisoning.

᎒᎒᎒

During the summers, I sometimes hired third year veterinary students to work with me while they were on vacation. One summer, I had a student working with me. He was a local boy, the son of one of my farm clients.

I went on a farm call and left Wayne at the office. When I returned he said, "I've got something in the back for you to see," and led me to one of the cages where we kept dogs that were in for grooming. There, out like a light with a syringe taped to one of her front legs, lay Penny, an oversized, overweight Miniature Pinscher dog.

"What happened?" I asked.

"Just after you left, Mr. Callender brought her in and, she was convulsing. He said he had been putting poison peanuts into mole holes and had dropped one. Penny immediately ate it. He knew the peanuts were laced with strychnine, so he grabbed Penny and jumped in the car to bring her here."

Wayne knew what had to be done, so he immediately injected Penny with an intravenous anesthetic.

"Thank goodness you were here," I said. "or Penny would have died."

Mr. Callender wasn't Penny's owner. She belonged to his mother-in-law, Mrs. McLeod.

Penny was brought to the hospital around ten a. m. It is a known fact that a dog poisoned by strychnine must be kept under anesthesia for sixteen to eighteen hours before the effects wear off. That would mean that Penny would need to be kept anesthetized until around two a.m.

I had no desire to stay at my hospital until two a. m. So at six p.m. when we went home for the night, I placed Penny in a blanket lined cardboard box and took her home with me.

When I walked through our backdoor carrying a cardboard box, Mary Jane asked, "What's in the box?"

"A dog."

"What are you going to do with it?"

"Sleep with it."

"In our bed?"

"In our room."

"What's wrong with the dog?"

It is doubtful she would have ever questioned anything I did to save an animal.

I explained the situation and told her I would place the box next to the head of our bed, so that when the dog started to convulse, I could inject her with more anesthetic.

This worked well. When the effects of the anesthetic began to wear off, Penny would begin to shake, and the vibrations of the box would wake me up. I would give her enough anesthetic to calm her down and then go back to sleep. She awakened me only twice after I went to bed. The next morning, she was awake and her normal self.

When Mr. Callender phoned to inquire about Penny the next morning, we were happy to be able to tell him she could go home.

CHAPTER 30

Wisdom from Kids

When I was a veterinary student at the University of Illinois, I worked part time for Dr. Kenton Kendall, a professor of dairy science. We were doing research to attempt to find the cause of parturient paresis (milk fever) which occurs shortly after calving in some high producing dairy cows.

Part of my job was to draw blood samples from suspect cows at various times prior to and after they gave birth to a calf at the U of I dairy barns.

Once, when a cow delivered her calf on Sunday I took our small daughter, Susan, with me to collect a blood sample because I wanted her to see a newborn calf.

Susan minded well and stood where I asked her while I drew blood from the jugular vein of the cow. The cow had not passed her placenta (afterbirth) yet, so it was hanging out of the vulva and was almost touching the floor.

We took the blood sample to the refrigerator in Dr. Kendall's laboratory at the Dairy Science Building before returning home.

When we arrived home, I said to Susan, "Tell mommy what you saw at the dairy barn."

Instead of saying that she saw a baby calf as I thought she would, she said, "I saw a cow with two tails."

꩜꩜꩜

On a Saturday afternoon, when I was interning with Dr. Strahler, I was sent to remove a retained placenta from a dairy cow.

When I arrived at the place he had sent me, I could see that here was a family that was enjoying the good life.

The house had once been a one room school house. However, the present owners had added on a couple of rooms, resided and reroofed it and made a very nice home for their family. The total size of the property was one acre. In addition to improving the house, the owners had built a small shed to house the cow, a calf, and one or two hogs which they would fatten and butcher for their meat supply.

I assumed that one or both of the parents worked in a nearby city, but they wanted their two young boys to grow up in the country, and that is what I meant by "living the good life." I would judge the boys were about eight and ten years old.

There were also a few hens to provide eggs for the family and a garden as well.

When I got out of the car, I handed the lady a pail and asked her for some warm water.

We walked to the shed where the cow was tied. As soon as the water was brought from the house, I donned my shoulder length obstetrical sleeve and lubricated it well before inserting my arm into the vaginal canal.

My hand had no more than cleared the lips of the vulva when one of boys nudged the other and said, "Look, he has his hand in the tunnel of love."

It was all I could do to keep from bursting out laughing, but fortunately I retained my aplomb and finished the job.

꩜꩜꩜

I remember when I was a child; I wasn't allowed to see an animal give birth to young until I had hogs of my own for an FFA project, so

I determined to allow our children to learn about the facts of life at a young age. According to my parents, a cow never had a calf; she "found a calf."

When our son, Tommy, was about three years old, I took him with me when I went on a farm call to deliver pigs from a sow that was having a difficult delivery.

We were at the farm for some time, because after I delivered a pig, I would have to wait for the sow to move the next pig far enough back where I could reach it.

Tommy was very patient for a three year old and seemed interested in what was going on.

When we arrived home, the first thing Tommy did was call out to his sister, "Hey, Suz, I know where pigs come from."

Susan responded with, "Where?"

Tommy said, "Somewhere between the back and the bottom," bent over, pointed to his rump and said, "Right there."

❧❧❧❧

When our two boys were small and went on farm calls with me, they wore boots and coveralls just like mine.

One day, they went with me to vaccinate pigs against cholera and erysipelas. The farrowing house we would be working in had a foundation which was about fifteen inches high. Since the foundation was about eight inches wide and the walls were only six inches wide, it made an ideal place for the boys to lean against as they held pigs for me to vaccinate.

I showed Tommy and Jimmy how to hold the pigs by the back legs with their bellies facing me as they squeezed the pigs between their legs for control. I handed Jimmy a pig small enough for him to handle and, at first, he had a good hold on it. Then, while squeezing the pig's body between his legs, he let go of the rear legs, looked at his hands and said, "But, Dad, you get all dirty."

I said, "Never mind, just hold the pigs."

Apparently my wife agreed with the part about getting all dirty, because when we got home, she made both the boys undress in the garage before allowing them in the house to take a shower.

Tommy was with me on a call to clamp and vaccinate calves one day when, after we finished, we were invited into the house for cake and drinks.

After we had finished our snacks, the lady of the house asked, "Tommy, would you like to take a piece of cake to Susan and Jimmy?"

Tommy very seriously replied, "Yes, and one for Mommy, too, please."

To say I was embarrassed is an understatement.

However, the lady of the house thought he was such a nice little boy to think of his mother.

Both our boys played Little League baseball. When Tommy was in his first year and was playing in what we called the minor league, I went on Saturday to watch his team practice.

As I stood along the fence, near one of the dugouts that surrounded the ball field, I noticed that the little boy in left field was holding his glove. His dad was near me, so I said, "Ed, Ryan doesn't have his glove on."

Ed immediately yelled, "Ry, put your glove on."

"Can't," Ryan hollered in return.

"Why not?" Ed asked.

"Got a bee in it," Ryan replied.

When Jimmy started playing Little League baseball the next year, I was standing at the fence next to the dugout of his team watching the game. Nine year old Jimmy was playing right field.

The first base coach of the opposing team came over to me and said, "Doc, I think Jimmy needs to go to the bathroom. He keeps shifting from foot to foot."

I said, "George, why don't you call time and go out and ask him?"

He said, "Okay."

George asked the umpire for time out, walked out into right field, and said something to Jimmy.

Jimmy shrugged his shoulders and said something to George. George turned around and returned to the infield.

As George drew near to where I was standing, I asked, "What did he say?"

George replied, "He said he's bored because no one ever hits a ball to him."

♩♩♩♩

When our children were small, we decided to take them to the county fair. As we were preparing to leave late in the afternoon, the phone rang.

Since we were dressed and ready to go, I was tempted to not answer but apparently my sense of duty overcame that notion.

The caller was Don Logan, a cattle raiser whom I had done little work for. He had an Angus heifer that had just delivered her calf. The calf was born dead, and the heifer could not stand.

I knew what her problem was -- she was suffering from obturator paralysis. The obturator nerves descend from the spine to the legs by passing through the pelvis. There is an opening on either side of the pelvis, and the nerves pass through this soft tissue. When a young heifer's birth canal is too small for the calf, and the cow struggles a long time to give birth, the nerves are damaged, usually temporarily. Eventually the heifer is able to rise and stand and usually returns to normal.

Since stopping at Don's farm on the way to the fair would only add about ten miles to the trip to the fairgrounds, I told him I would stop and look at her on our way.

When we arrived, we saw the heifer with the afterbirth in the grass about six feet behind her. About three feet past the afterbirth lay the dead calf.

The heifer was lying on her sternum with her feet under her and appeared alert and had moved about nine feet from where she had delivered the calf.

As I walked up to her, she made a half-hearted attempt to rise.

I explained the situation to Don and told him I felt she would stand in a few days.

In the meantime, he needed to provide her with hay and fresh water at all times. The only medicine he need give her was the "tincture of time and patience."

When I got back into the car, my wife told me that our son, Tommy, had seen the calf and afterbirth lying there and said, "Mommy, look at the calf's pajama pants behind him."

ﾑﾑﾑ

I can recall when there was a practice of passing out cigars and candy bars when one got married, or when one's wife had a baby. Cigars for men who smoked and candy bars for women, children, and men who didn't smoke.

I don't recall the occasion, or who gave it to me, but I had a cigar. As I was driving to a farm call, I took it out of my pocket and lit it.

When I did that our three year old son Jimmy, who was along for the ride asked, "You got one of those for me?"

CHAPTER **31**

The Goodwells

Cool evening in early March….just right for a farm animal to have a birthing problem. As if the telephone could read my mind, it rang. Answering it I heard….

"Dr. Day, I haven't called you before, but I need you badly. I have a cow that is having difficulty calving. I phoned my vet, but he's at a school board meeting and won't leave to come out and help us. Oh, by the way, I'm Mike Goodwell."

I asked for and received directions to the Goodwell farm and was on my way.

When I arrived, I was greeted by the father and two strapping high school boys, both about six feet tall. We shook hands all around and they helped me carry my equipment into the barn. A pail of warm water was sitting there waiting for me.

I surveyed the situation. The Angus beef cow had her head in a stanchion in what obviously had been a dairy barn at one time. I could see two feet protruding from the vulva and the bottoms of the hooves were on top. This meant the calf was coming breech because the feet I was looking at were hind feet. The cow was standing with her feet in the gutter used for the run off of urine, and this should have been a warning to me, but the light bulb did not come on. Her rear feet were lower than her front feet, and a little later I would see the results from this.

I placed the straps around the lower legs of the calf and then situated the fetal extractor properly. As I held the strap of the fetal extractor over the cow's back to keep it from slipping, the older boy, Ted, operated the fetal extractor. As soon as the hips exited the vulva, the rest of the calf slid out easily. The calf, lying on the floor of the barn, was not breathing. It did have a heartbeat, however.

I had noticed some harness pegs on the wall, used in the time when draft horses were the principal mode of power on the farm.

I said to the boys, "Quick, let's hang the strap over one of those harness pegs." We did, and I was rubbing and slapping the calf's rib cage to get it to breath. Mucus was running out of the calf's nose and mouth. The calf took one breath, then a second, and then I heard it. Plop!!

I turned to see what had caused the plopping sound. The cow had everted her uterus. She had continued to strain after we delivered the calf and because her rear feet were lower than her front ones, had turned her uterus wrong side out, and it was hanging like a big tube of bologna below her vulva.

We lowered the now breathing calf to the floor and turned our attention to the everted uterus. I issued each young man, Ted and Rick, a pair of plastic shoulder length obstetrical sleeves and asked them to hold the uterus in place while I attempted to replace it to its proper position in the body.

We had properly lubricated the uterus before attempting to replace it, so the surface was nice and slick. I cautioned the two teenagers that the uterus was not as tough as a basketball so they needed to be gentle with it.

It took about ten minutes for us to replace the uterus. I then placed two sulfa urea boluses deep into the uterus and sutured the lips of the vulva together with an x suture of umbilical tape. As an afterthought, I injected the cow with a small dose of oxytocin to cause the uterus to contract.

After instructing the Goodwells on how to remove the sutures in seven days, I got in my car and drove the fourteen miles to a nice warm bed.

I was on the Goodwell farm many, many times over the next thirty-nine years, but one other visit really stands out in my mind.

Again, it was early spring, and it was a birthing problem...only this time it was a ewe having a problem delivering her lamb(s).

I was down on my knees behind the ewe trying to manipulate the lamb out through the vaginal canal, only this time, there were three sons watching me along with father Mike. The youngest son, Jack, was about seven years old.

As I brought the first lamb into the world, I heard Jack ask his father, "Dad, how did that lamb get in there?" Mike didn't answer.

As I was working to deliver the second lamb, once again I heard, "Dad, how did that lamb get in there?"

I looked up at Mike and saw that his face had gotten red, but he didn't respond to the question.

And then I heard, "Doc, how did that lamb get in there?"

Again, I looked up at Mike, and he slowly nodded his head yes.

So I said," Jack, you know that when your Dad wants corn to grow he plants seed in the ground."

Jack nodded yes.

"You know that you have an old buck sheep around here, right?"

Jack said, "Right."

"When the buck sheep wants lambs to grow, he plants seeds in the ewes."

"Okay, Doc, but how did that hole get in there?"

"Well, Jack, the hole is always there, but it gets larger when it's time for the lambs to be born."

Mike said, "Jack, it's your bedtime, you had better go to the house."

I didn't learn about this until Ted told me many years later, but Jack went in the house and told his mother all that had happened in the barn.

Ted also told me that at "Show and Tell" the next day at school, Jack was telling his second grade classmates what he had observed the previous night. When he had gone so far in his story, his teacher said, "Jack, I think that's enough."

And Jack replied, "Oh no, I'm just getting to the good part."

CHAPTER 32

Birds of a Feather

When I graduated from the University Of Illinois College Of Veterinary Medicine, I felt ill equipped to treat birds -- be they canaries or Barred Rock laying hens. It is true that we received a course in poultry pathology, but this only taught us how to diagnose a disease outbreak in a flock of poultry, that is, chickens or turkeys. This diagnosis was done on dead birds, not live ones.

So far as the care and treatment of pet birds, I knew very little. It's true that we were required to clean the cages of the three or four parakeets and canaries that were kept in the waiting room of the small animal clinic. It was also true that we had a filthy mouthed Mina bird in the isolation room of the clinic. He had quite a vocabulary such as an emphatic, "Not here!!" when one of the clinician instructors was paged over the loud speaker system. He also managed to give out a lusty "Hey, Doc," when one of us students walked into the room.

Next door to the small animal clinic was the Fine and Applied Arts Building. Often in the spring, or early fall, some of the students would sit under the trees and do their homework. If the windows were open, the Mina would sit on his perch in his cage, look out at the students and yell obscenities that students before my class's time had taught him.

My training in poultry pathology was put to use only twice during my nearly forty years of practice. On one occasion, I diagnosed the avian leukosis complex in a flock of laying hens and on another occasion, I diagnosed worms in a farm flock.

❧❧❧

So, I wasn't really prepared for what I found when Bill Breckner walked into my waiting room one cold November afternoon. I was in one of my exam rooms with a patient, but I could see he had something under his coat.

As soon as I finished with the dog I was treating, I walked out into the waiting room and said, "What do you have under your coat, Bill?"

"I'm not sure, Doc," he said as he walked into the exam room.

I closed both doors to the exam room so that whatever he had would not get away when he unzipped his coat. As soon as he opened up his coat, I knew that I had never seen a bird like this. I was positive he was some species of raptor…I just didn't know what species.

As Bill opened his coat and placed a very docile bird on the table, I could see the bird weighed about three pounds and was approximately two feet long. His beak was yellow and there was a band of red flesh above the beak, sort of like the red on the head of a turkey vulture, but smoother.

I asked Bill how he came to have this bird in his possession, and he replied that he was harvesting soybeans at a farm west of town. He saw the bird hunkered down in a fence row on his first trip and continued to watch him each time he passed. After the fourth pass, he decided to bring the bird to me.

I felt of both of the bird's legs and his wings and could find no fractures. One of his eyes appeared bright; his other was gray indicating he was blind. I had no idea how old he was, but I thought him to be aged.

I told Bill I thought the bird was suffering from exposure and was just plain cold. I suggested that I take him back to the cage room and keep him overnight for observation.

The bird sat quietly in the rear of the cage where I placed him. I then put a small heavy crockery bowl of water in front of him.

I returned to the front of the building to continue my office hours. However, I instructed one of my assistants to check on the bird periodically.

There was little change in the bird's attitude when we left the hospital after office hours at six p. m.

After my family had finished eating our evening meal, I got out one of our bird books to see what species of bird we had in my clinic.

It didn't take long to determine the bird was a Crested Caracara, or Mexican Eagle, the national bird of Mexico. According to the book I read, the bird was a cross between an eagle and a vulture and a cousin to the falcon. The book also indicated that the bird ate snakes, lizards and other small live prey as well as dead animals.

When I read that the bird's natural range was Florida, Texas, Arizona, and Mexico and on down into Central America, I was puzzled as to how the bird came to be in Illinois. I guess there was no answer other than he had been blown this far north by winds. Or, perhaps he had been held in captivity by someone in the north and got away. I guess we'll never know.

Upon arriving at my animal hospital the next morning, I found a totally different bird. When I walked into the cage room and peered into the cage holding the bird, he was very alert and even flapped his wings.

I was then confronted with another problem. He had several bowel movements during the night and needed to have his cage cleaned. It was one thing to handle the bird when he was cold and depressed, but would be quite different in his present mood.

I finally decided on my modus operandi. I would open another cage door across the aisle, don my elbow length lead lined x-ray gloves, open the door to his cage, grab him, transport him to the other cage, release him and hope he wouldn't get away before I closed the cage door. My plan worked, and the bird was now in a clean cage with fresh water.

I decided, since I did not have any snakes, lizards, or dead animals for him to feed on, hamburger would have to suffice as his diet.

When one of my employees arrived at work, I asked her to take some money from our petty cash and go to the grocery store for hamburger.

When she returned, she and I headed for the cage room armed with a pound of hamburger and an English capsule forceps. I intended to roll the hamburger into small balls and deposit the balls through the bars of the cage with the forceps. An English capsule forceps is somewhat like a pair of tongs and is used to place small boluses or pills far back in a calf's mouth so he will swallow them. By feeding the bird this way, I hoped to save my fingers.

The hamburger was just what the doctor ordered. That bird gobbled each ball up as soon as we placed it in the cage. We fed about a half pound of hamburger to the bird, and he was still eager to eat, but I didn't want to feed so much at one time that we upset his digestive system. Who knows how long it had been since he had eaten.

We moved the bird to a clean cage, gave him fresh water, and fed him the remainder of the hamburger before we left for home that evening. As before, he immediately ate the meat we placed before him.

How were we going to get out of the dilemma we were in? The bird's bill for room and board was mounting with each day he spent with us and, as far as I could see, the bird had no visible means of support. And yet, we couldn't turn him back out into the cold, nor could we drive down to Texas to free him in his own habitat.

And then I had an idea. I had met Dr. Les Fisher, veterinarian and curator of the Lincoln Park Zoo in Chicago at a veterinary seminar, so I felt comfortable phoning him to ask if the zoo would accept a Caracara.

When I reached him, told him the story and posed the question to him, he readily agreed to take the bird, but allowed they didn't have the funds to come down and get him. I immediately said, "No matter, we'll bring the bird to you."

On Sunday, after church, I placed the bird in a small wire dog cage, set the cage in the back of our station wagon, and our family went for a ninety mile Sunday outing to deliver the bird to the zoo. The trip allowed me to get rid of a freeloading bird and enabled our children to have an afternoon of entertainment watching the animals.

♪♪♪

My next wild bird experience involved a much larger bird -- a Great Blue Heron, and it happened like this:

I was called to the farm of Lonnie Graves on Labor Day to re-move a retained placenta (afterbirth) from a cow. Most cows pass the afterbirth shortly after delivering their calf, but occasionally, for some reason, a cow fails to get rid of hers. Ordinarily, I would not have made this call on a holiday, but it had already been three days since the cow had delivered her calf. Forty-eight hours after calving is the optimal time to remove a retained placenta because it is easier to unbutton the placenta at that time. It is also early enough that the cow won't yet be infected. So, not wanting to let the cow go another day, I went to the farm on a holiday.

Donning my shoulder length plastic obstetrical sleeve I proceed-ed to remove the placenta by unbuttoning it from the uterus. A bovine placenta has cotyledons (buttons) attached to it. These buttons, in turn, attach to the caruncles which are part of the uterus. There are many cotyledons and caruncles in the placenta and uterine wall. The cotyledons attach to the caruncles in much the same way two pieces of Velcro stick together.

After removing the placenta and placing two sulfa boluses deep into the uterus to prevent infection, I removed the lariat from the cow's neck and let her back out into the cow lot with the other cows.

Just as I finished washing up and putting my lariat and obstetrical lubricant back into my vehicle, Lonnie said, "I've got another job for you."

"What's that?" I asked.

"Just follow me," he replied without any explanation.

I followed him up toward his house, and just outside the back porch I saw a fairly large wooden crate made out of slats that appeared to have a large bird in it.

As I got closer and closer to the crate, I could see that the bird was a Great Blue Heron. Lonnie reached down and grabbed a piece of fish line and pulled the bird's bill out through a space between the boards of the crate. I could see the barb end of a fish hook protruding from inside the lower bill.

"I need you to remove that fish hook," said Lonnie.

"Do you have a pair of side cutters?" I asked.

"I'll get 'em," he answered.

When Lonnie returned with the pliers, I asked him, "How did you catch this bird? "

"I have a trotline in the river down behind the farm. Apparently he liked the bait I had on the hooks."

A trotline is a heavy fish line that stretches across a river or creek to which shorter lines with hooks are attached. Fishermen check them daily to see if a catch has been made.

When Lonnie had checked his line earlier that the morning, instead of a fish, he had caught the bird. He cut the line and led the bird up to the house like one would lead a horse or cow with a halter and rope.

I grasped the fish line to pull the heron's head through the gap in the wood and cut the barb off of the hook. This made it easy to pull the shaft of the hook out of the bill.

Lonnie removed the back of the crate; the bird backed out, and sedately walked away.

❧❧❧

It was my habit to stop mid-morning for coffee and a donut at the local "Donut Station," so named because the business occupied what had once been a Shell gas station. It was winter, and the temperature was about twenty degrees Fahrenheit.

One morning after I had my coffee, as I exited the door to go to my vehicle, I noticed a very small bird sitting on the trunk of one of the parked cars. I went back into the building and asked whose car was sitting right by the door. When one of the men answered, I asked "Do you know there's a small bird sitting on your trunk?" He said, "Yes, he's ridden there all the way from home." "And how far is that?" I asked. "About seven miles."

"He's suffering from the cold," I told the man and then asked if he would allow me to take the bird to my hospital to warm him up. "Go right ahead, he's not my bird," he answered.

I walked over to the car's trunk, reached down and picked the bird up and carried him to my vehicle. He was so cold, he didn't move.

Arriving at my hospital, I carried the little bird into the area where we did our dog grooming and placed him in one of the holding cages. Unfortunately, I didn't place a towel or paper over the bars in the cage. A couple of hours later, the bird warmed up. He flew through the bars of the cage door into one of our storerooms. The top shelf held boxes of supplies such as gauze and tape. Since the top was open on one of the boxes, the bird flew into that box, so it was an easy matter to catch him again. Before we placed the bird in the cage, we covered the barred door with a bath towel to prevent his escaping again.

In the meantime, we had identified the bird as a golden crowned kinglet and learned that kinglets like evergreen trees.

By the time I went home for lunch, the sun had come out and the temperature had risen to above forty degrees, so I took the bird with me. We have a large blue spruce tree in our back yard. I went out the back door of the garage and released the bird about ten feet from the spruce tree. He immediately flew into the tree, and that's the last I saw of him.

♪♪♪♪

My wife was a reading teacher in our school district for many years. She taught at a grade school in a small town about five miles south of our town for one or two years.

There were two young first year teachers in the same school and they owned a young cockatiel. One morning when they awoke, they found a very depressed bird sitting on the bottom of the cage. On their way to work, they dropped the bird off at my hospital. They were in such a hurry that I didn't have time to examine the bird while they were present.

When I did examine the bird, I found her to be egg bound. She was trying to lay an egg, but couldn't.

As I mentioned at the beginning of this chapter, I was sorely lacking in the knowledge of avian medicine. However, I learned somewhere and somehow that in treating an egg bound bird, one should never break an egg while it is in the cloaca.

The usual treatment of an egg bound bird at that time was to infuse a small amount of mineral oil into the bird's cloaca, wait awhile and then gently apply pressure to the lower abdomen and thus force the egg out of the cloaca.

I am sure that in this day of newer knowledge about birds and advanced technology, there are improved ways of treating the condition.

So, several times during the day, I used the mineral oil to treat the bird, and then gently applied pressure to her abdomen, trying to force the egg out. Each of these times, I failed.

Finally, about three o'clock in the afternoon (I knew I could expect the owners to arrive at any minute) I infused mineral oil into the cloaca again. Then I applied gentle pressure (or so I thought) and squeezed gently on the bird's lower abdomen.

"Oh! No!" Or at least I think that's what I said.

The egg had burst and yolk was dripping out of the bird. That was a mistake I had been trying to avoid.

Once again, I infused mineral oil into the cloaca. Then came the soft lining of the egg. THERE WAS NO SHELL!! As they say in the Alka Seltzer commercials, "Oh what a relief" it was to know that I had not injured the bird in trying to help her.

When the owners came to inquire about the bird about an hour later, she was sitting on her perch and very alert.

They were quite impressed with my treatment of their bird. I didn't have the heart to tell them I was just plain lucky.

Sometimes the birds presented to me were not alive. To wit, one morning when I arrived at my hospital, I found a dead bird on my front doorstep. No note, no card saying who owned the bird, just a dead bird.

I carried the bird into my examination room and laid it on the table. I was in a quandary. I didn't know the owner, didn't know the cause of death, but more importantly, I didn't know what was expected of me. Perhaps someone just wanted me to dispose of the bird.

About an hour later, my phone rang and a voice on the other end asked, "Did you find my bird?"

"Yes, what am I supposed to do with it?" I asked.

"I want you to tell me what sex it is."

"You want me to sex a dead bird. Why, pray tell?"

"We had two birds, and they were supposed to be a male and a female, and we want to raise birds. Our cat killed this bird and we want to know if she killed the male or the female so we can buy the proper sex to replace it."

Then I asked the question I should have asked earlier, "Who is this?"

"Terry Thomas."

"Well, Terry, I don't even know how to sex a live bird, let alone a dead one."

"You don't? Who can I get to sex it?"

I replied, "Why don't you call the University of Illinois small animal clinic?"

"Good idea."

About an hour later, I heard from Terry again. "Go ahead and dispose of the bird," he said. "The people of the U of I said it's impossible to sex a dead bird."

I wasn't surprised at something like this from Terry. Once, he had told me he was going to buy semen and artificially inseminate his sows.

"How are you going to store the semen?" I asked.

"In the refrigerator," he replied.

"No, Terry," I explained, "you need a nitrogen tank to keep the semen frozen until you use it."

That was the end of Terry's idea of artificially breeding his sows.

⟆⟆⟆

Woodcarving is a hobby of mine. I have carved items as small as an elephant three-quarters of an inch long and a half-inch high to a rocking horse eighteen inches high and twenty-four inches long. The rockers were additional.

Once, I carved a blue jay, took it to work and laid it on one the examination tables. I'm not sure why I took it to my office, but it was probably to show a fellow woodcarver. He was scheduled to bring his dog in for a rabies vaccination any day.

I was in the kennel room when one of my employees came to work. As she came into the room where I was checking on a dog, she asked, "What's with the dead bird in the exam room?"

That question made me feel pretty good because it was in indication that my carvings of birds were realistic.

⟆⟆⟆

Three summers ago, during an ambitious moment, I was down on my hands and knees cleaning leaves and debris from under shrubs in our front yard. In order to rest a bit, I sat back on my haunches.

It was then I saw two fledgling wrens flitting about the shrubbery, testing their ability to fly. Their home was a log cabin bird house hanging in a Sunset Red maple tree I had planted for my wife about thirty years ago.

As I rested, I was surveying the area to the south of our house. Across the street was a Lutheran Church; farther to the southeast was a grade school and beyond that a cornfield with plants about knee high.

Presently, I felt something touch down on my right shoulder. Was it a baby wren? Or was it a twig that had wafted down from the maple tree?

I sat there for what seemed minutes, but probably was only mere seconds. Finally, I turned my head to the right to see. It was then the baby wren flew off to test its wings some more.

At church on Sunday, I asked our pastor if he could give some meaning to the little wren's landing on my shoulder.

He interpreted it as the Lord's way of acknowledging that I had nurtured and healed his creatures for the better part of my life.

CPSIA information can be obtained at www.ICGtesting.com
Printed in the USA
LVOW06*0042160914

404217LV00001B/1/P

9 781478 734833